UNDERCOVER
Bag Lady

An Exposé of Christian Attitudes
Toward the Homeless

Kimberly Bowman

UNDERCOVER BAG LADY: AN EXPOSÉ OF CHRISTIAN ATTITUDES TOWARD THE HOMELESS

1405 SW 6th Avenue • Ocala, Florida 34471 • Phone 352-622-1825 • Fax 352-622-1875
Website: www.atlantic-pub.com • Email: sales@atlantic-pub.com
SAN Number: 268-1250

Library of Congress Cataloging-in-Publication Data

Names: Bowman, Kimberly (Undercover Bag Lady), author.
Title: Undercover bag lady : an expos?e of Christian attitudes toward the homeless / by Kimberly
    Bowman.
Description: Ocala : Atlantic Publishing Group, Inc., 2019.
Identifiers: LCCN 2018057260 (print) | LCCN 2019004317 (ebook) | ISBN 9781620236307
    (Ebook) | ISBN 9781620236307 (pbk.) | ISBN 1620236303
Subjects: LCSH: Church work with the homeless.
Classification: LCC BV4456 (ebook) | LCC BV4456 .B69 2019 (print) | DDC 261.8/3250975676—
    dc23 LC record available at https://lccn.loc.gov/2018057260

Printed in the United States

PROJECT MANAGER: Katie Cline
INTERIOR LAYOUT AND JACKET DESIGN: Nicole Sturk

Over the years, we have adopted a number of dogs from rescues and shelters. First there was Bear and after he passed, Ginger and Scout. Now, we have Kira, another rescue. They have brought immense joy and love not just into our lives, but into the lives of all who met them.

We want you to know a portion of the profits of this book will be donated in Bear, Ginger and Scout's memory to local animal shelters, parks, conservation organizations, and other individuals and nonprofit organizations in need of assistance.

*— **Douglas & Sherri Brown,***
President & Vice-President of Atlantic Publishing

To Mom and Dad

TABLE OF CONTENTS

You own everything that happened to you.
Tell your stories.
If people wanted you to write warmly about them,
they should have behaved better.

ANNE LAMOTT

INTRODUCTION

The beginning of my journey toward transforming into the Undercover Bag Lady began when I was just an inquisitive teenager in the early 1980s. Being a self-proclaimed shock-value enthusiast and an avid viewer of hidden-camera TV shows like "Candid Camera", the prospect of hiding myself in plain view and observing society's mannerisms has always intrigued me. There's nothing quite like catching someone off guard and discovering what really makes them tick. To that end, I'm inclined to suspect that I missed my calling as an actress, for I truly do believe that the world is a stage, and we have but a brief season to give the performance of a lifetime.

Fast-forward 35 years, and this Michigan girl found herself in the Bible Belt with nothing but the insipidity of time on her hands. My recently retired husband and I had spontaneously decided to relocate to the beautiful state of North Carolina to begin a new life at the quintessential start of our golden years. Suddenly, I was a stranger in a strange land with no friends and absolutely nothing constructive with which to keep myself occupied.

Even with a love of all things retail and a plethora of emporiums and boutiques from which to choose, there was only so much bargain-hunting even a devoted shopper like myself could do before ennui set in. Two months into this idle existence, and my golden years were fast becoming dull and monotonous. It was time to either begin popping Prozac or find a meaningful, engaging project I could sink my teeth into. The latter plan seemed more rational than the former. It didn't take me long to realize that, with a little effort and planning, my lifelong dream of analyzing human nature from a hidden vantage point could become a reality. Undercover Bag Lady would soon be born.

After working with the homeless community in various capacities over the span of three decades, I sincerely assumed that I knew everything there was to know about them; pretending to be one in their ranks would be no great feat. However, I quickly learned that no amount of food distribution could teach me the actual burden on these people, and no length of time participating in blanket drives could prepare me emotionally for my role as an actual homeless woman.

During my time as the Undercover Bag Lady, I visited 10 vastly different Christian-based churches incognito and took note of my experiences. I then wrote this book to relate my first-hand experiences and expose the good, the bad, and the ugly. The Undercover Bag Lady story unfolds over an eight-week period during which time I characterized myself as a homeless bag lady named Jean and darkened the doors of unsuspecting churches with the purpose of chronicling their reactions.

"Undercover Bag Lady" is a journey of self-discovery, as well as an exposé of the human condition. My mission was a quest to offer a challenge to the faith of those who profess goodness. As a significantly unusual aspiration was checked off my bucket list, I personally learned the intrinsic human need to be loved and accepted, regardless of one's rank in society. And I found that love and acceptance is sometimes given in the least likely of places and in the most unexpected forms.

Because I do not wish to embarrass or malign any specific individual or local assembly, the actual names of those I came in contact with during my time as the Bag Lady are being withheld at my discretion. For this reason, I will simply refer to a specific church by denomination and will say that all houses of worship mentioned in my book reside in the comfortable suburbs of Charlotte, North Carolina.

May my book raise some much-needed awareness for the plight of the homeless everywhere and be a compelling voice for those whose voices are ignored.

CHAPTER ONE

My Catholic Encounter

If you cannot find Christ in the beggar at the church door,
you will not find him in the chalice.

—SAINT JOHN CHRYSOSTOM

I was raised in a devout, Roman-Catholic family — Catechism, weekly Mass, the works. As an oddly analytical child, I recall my maternal grandmother earnestly praying her rosary for seemingly endless hours, the shiny glass beads silently beckoning a call to holy reverence. During her prayer time, Grandma refused to allow me to turn on the television, so I resorted to subdued play with my Barbie dolls while impatiently watching the clock. Her lips whispered the words to the Our Father and Hail Mary effortlessly, a repetitive ritual she performed without fail for decades — one my young mind could never quite grasp. *Precisely what was the point of praying the same prayers over and over again? Didn't saying it once get the job done?*

Saturday afternoon Mass was an absolute mandate; attendance was not optional. To *not* attend Mass would have been sinful, an act of heresy, practically. Even back then I admitted that I could use all the Sacraments I could get, as I carefully stored them up for a rainy day in the event I did something dreadful in the future that made God *really* mad. My imaginary friends were priests and nuns. Actually, one priest, who was the personification of an all-patient, loving father similar to Ward Cleaver, and two nuns — one good-natured like Mary Poppins, the other as mean as The Wicked Witch of the West. (To this day I'm certain there is a potent psychological significance to my choice of fictional playmates; if I allowed myself to delve deep enough I'm sure my therapist would have a field day.) And my fondest spiritual childhood memory was wearing an angelic white dress and veil for my First Communion — I glowed like a radiant bride! It was a day unparalleled to any other, because I felt ceremoniously married to God, a sacred union I naively trusted would help me piously stay the religious course for all the days of my life.

Perhaps it was this original affinity that was my principal incentive for choosing the Catholic Church on my initial run as the Bag Lady. It felt like coming home. Only this time I found myself to be the rebellious prodigal child who no longer fit in with the family. I was the disobedient, wayward daughter who had squandered her years in unorthodox living and was returning home, shamefully begging for mercy. The lifelong estrangement to the Church would no doubt be a stumbling block.

For several weeks prior to my Bag Lady debut my husband, Gary, and I carried out "covert missions" as we scoped out potential churches and appraised prospective locations. Sunday mornings would find us scouting quiet neighborhoods, learning the schedule of worship services, and watching the rhythm of the churches' faithful from afar. We became so good at it that I was tempted to change our names to John Steed and Emma Peel, the voguish secret agents and masters of espionage from the 1960s British hit television series "The Avengers." To remain inconspicuous, I even dressed the part by wearing all-black outfits, although I must confess I never did pull off the sultry spy image quite as well as Diana Rigg.

My objective was to target a variety of unsuspecting candidate churches from every denomination available locally, then narrow down the playing field. Deciding which churches to include in my study was more laborious than originally anticipated, but it actually proved to be the easiest part of the project. After all, it was the Bible Belt for goodness' sake — my options were endless!

Scouring the internet, making anonymous phone calls, and performing trial runs became an essential part of the project's overall success. This phase took several weeks by itself and involved a great deal of scrutiny.

There were so many congregations to choose from, and I wanted to embrace variety everywhere I could, including location, worship style, and the number in attendance. The definitive list was handpicked and researched meticulously prior to the final selection. But even with all the time invested in the analysis, I realized that choosing churches was invariably just a crapshoot. In the end, fate makes its own decisions, no matter what.

Gary and I planned out our strategy and memorized our movements down to a tee; if I'd worn a watch, we might have even synchronized them. I'd be stealthily dropped off at an undisclosed location in close proximity to the church and then approach the building solo. I didn't want to do anything that would jeopardize my cover, so I had to give the illusion of showing up alone. Alone — that's something the homeless are good at being; the lonely solitary drifter who relies on no one, believes no one, trusts no one. I had to become that person.

On these Sundays, while I drifted up to the week's church, Gary would park the car and quietly and casually approach the church from a different direction, posing as a random visitor. We decided there were definite benefits to his presence during the church visits. From his position as a respectable, inconspicuous member of the congregation, Gary was able to discreetly take pictures of me on his phone when the opportunity presented itself.

Tensions ran high that first Saturday evening. I was as nervous as I was excited. Part of me was worried that these last minute jitters would scare me into backing down from my self-imposed commitment, so weeks beforehand, I secretly revealed my project to several close family members and friends. I knew that personal accountability would help motivate me to stay the course or, at the very least scare me out of withdrawing at the eleventh hour. This was good thinking on my part, because as anxious as I was that Saturday night, I'd have ducked out for sure without a reinforcement plan. Fortunately, everyone's encouragement provided me the boldness required to carry out my plan, even if there were those who inaudibly thought it to be somewhat eccentric.

Sleep eluded me that night, as I very well expected it would. Unfamiliar worries and unnerving scenarios played over and over in my head as the clock tauntingly ticked closer to my opening performance. Was I really going through with this? And if I did, what would happen to me? What consequences would await me if I discarded my true identity to willfully take up the role of a vagabond? Would I be treated badly or thrown from the front steps like an unwanted stray? Visions of being mercilessly hauled out of the church by disgruntled ushers threw me into further anxiety. As my mind reeled through the choppy waters of every conceivable potential disaster, I lay wide-awake in the menacing darkness, willing myself to sleep to no avail.

But as the Catholic Sunday dawned, I regarded my sleep-deprived, hassled visage and determined that the dark under-eye circles could only add to my weary homeless costume. In the demure privacy of my cozy master bathroom, I donned the items of my uniform that I'd purchased at a secondhand thrift store: a long, tattered khaki skirt over old-fashioned lilac-tinted polyester pants; a ratty, painted t-shirt over a flimsy, ruffled cream blouse; and, for the finishing touch, a well-worn, quilted red flannel hunting jacket. To give my clothes ragged authenticity, Gary and I had dragged them down rural dirt roads in the dead of night as they limply hung out of our car door.

Water was absolutely off limits as I performed what would become a Sunday morning ritual. In celebratory fashion, I threw caution to the wind, opening a plastic container of mud reserved especially for this day, and embellished my neck and clothes with remnants of damp sludge, digging my unkempt fingernails into the muck until my grimy hands told the tale of a life in ruins. Fluffing up my bed head hairdo, which I deliberately hadn't washed in a week, I added a dusting of baby powder to affect age and dullness. Slipping into a pair of shabby men's sneakers with hole-ridden toes and thin, black dollar-store winter gloves with the fingertips missing, my transformation was completed. And since I could hardly call myself "Bag Lady" without it, I stuffed a large, wrinkled shopping bag with more tattered bits of costumery.

Upon completion, I stood in front of the floor length mirror and stared at the strange, ragged woman standing in my bedroom. "You're certifiably nuts," I remarked to my ghastly reflection. But the time to turn back had passed. I was a newly christened homeless woman, and it was time to give life to Bag Lady.

The moment of truth dawned on that 28-degree morning as Gary dropped me off near the church on a secluded, tree-lined side road. With the leafless branches of the trees clattering in the frigid wind above, I climbed from the car feeling like the eyes of the world were watching and judging. As Gary disappeared in a fog of warm exhaust, I felt an overwhelming flood of loneliness that quickly turned to panic.

"What the hell am I doing?" I squeaked, shivering. It was January 7th, my birthday, and I was standing alone in the street, dressed as a homeless woman, and slowly turning to ice. Months of zealous preparation had been reduced to this, and self-doubt washed away weeks of confident planning, leaving me feeling like a mud-caked fraud playing dress-up. At this point, it felt more sensible to hurl myself over Niagara Falls in a barrel than to proceed with this ridiculous pursuit. I peered at the prodigious church in the distance and an ominous foreboding threatened my resolve.

It was the first Sunday of the new year and even a Michigander like myself could feel a frosty hand squeezing the breath out of me. For a split second, I regretted this whole bag lady idea and longed to be back at home, snug in my warm bed with my sweet pup curled up by my feet. Instead, I was voluntarily dressed as an impoverished beggar, wandering the frozen streets of upscale suburbia. This had to be the most ridiculous brainchild ever conceived.

Then, almost as if on cue, I remembered something I'd read a few days before: "This is the year I will be stronger, braver, kinder, and fiercer than ever!" With renewed determination, I took a deep breath of snow-scented air and emerged from the sheltering cover of the dense thicket. With each step of frozen ground crunching under my feet I thought *fierce, fierce, fierce* as I trudged on toward my precarious fate.

Right on schedule, I arrived 20 minutes before the first Mass was scheduled to begin. By nature's prompting, the shadows of early morning began to sleepily surrender to an ethereal sunrise. There were no birds chirping on this cold winter morning and not another human being was in sight. If this were any other scenario I could have fully appreciated God's masterful handiwork — a noiseless exhibition nevertheless bursting with vibrant hues — but tension and uncertainty stole the grandeur of the moment like an unrepentant thief. I sat against the stone ledge of a fountain in nervous preoccupation.

Because it was January, the fountain was not in operation, so my makeshift bench provided the perfect perch from which I could make contact with every parishioner that walked by. The fountain was in the center of the courtyard, so any visitor had to walk around me to enter the building. Bag Lady's shocking presence was fully evident to every person from this position.

As I waited for church members to arrive, I imagined how spectacular this fountain must be during summer, with its fresh streams inviting passersby to tarry a moment. I pictured children skimming their little hands through the wellspring of cool water as their mothers sternly warned them not to get their church clothes wet. But I was relieved that the majestic fountain was not functioning that morning, because the sight of my appalling reflection in its shimmering pool would have surely depressed me. In stark contrast to the enchanting fountain, Bag Lady was not such a welcome sight.

The procession began with gentle footsteps few and far between and a couple hasty glances thrown and retrieved as they beheld the pathetic figure stooped in their courtyard. Gradually the trickle of churchgoers became a steady, urgent stream, and the glances became unmasked stares of suspicion and nervousness.

Admitting that I was out of place would be a gross understatement. The worshippers wore everything from suits and ties with gleaming dress shoes to khakis, sweaters, and boots, yet even the shabbiest of the lot was a fashion mogul compared to my ramshackle appearance. I felt utterly ashamed and embarrassed. Some of the parishioners went out of their way to avoid me as much as possible, practically bumping into cement pillars in the process. It was as though I were living out a biblical parable as a wounded traveler pleading for a Good Samaritan to take pity or a pestilent leper with passersby taking careful strides to evade me at all costs. It felt painfully bizarre as the gravity of the scene unfolded before me.

As if in slow motion, occurrences that would ordinarily seem insignificant held such weight in the depth of the moment. A shunning glance, a hissing whisper, a wide berth — they all felt like slaps and shoves. But also in the weight of the moment were moments of sweet consolation: the sonorous hum of a car engine in the distance, the flash of sun on a young girl's black patent leather shoes, the fragrant musk of men's cologne. To escape from the discomfort of my situation, my mind was grasping at small, pleasant diversions. Thank God for the little things.

Then came the tipping point, and not a minute too soon. Sitting there discouraged and dejected, witnessing the rebuff of countless churchgoers as they hurried into the shelter of their house of worship, a new determination arose from my innermost being. That brave, fierce, unstoppable woman whom I longed to see emerged from somewhere deep within. In that moment, I found the courage I so desperately needed as self-doubt yielded to self-assurance. Denying the urge to fall into an abyss of humiliation, I was instantly aware that I possessed the ability to rise above my feeble insecurities and carry out this Bag Lady mission.

With renewed fervor, I embraced my role seriously, almost believing my own acting. *Today I am homeless, and I must shut out the rest of the world.* It was time to be Jean the Bag Lady, the wanderer, the nomad without a past, present, or future. I felt myself melt into the scenery like the invisible woman; in the world but not of it. Jean was my new identity. Kimberly no longer existed.

As the procession continued, sounding more like a funeral march than a hymn of welcome, part of me yearned to turn and run away while I still held a shred of self-dignity, but my tenacious stubbornness held me fixed. Jean doesn't run from a challenge.

In the space of a half hour, I counted 240 adults walk past me, typically with heads down, their eyes carefully averted as they entered the church.

Happy freaking birthday to me. Homeless people have birthdays, too, but they have no cake, no streamers and balloons, no presents wrapped in colorful paper and tied with beautiful bows. Never had I felt so isolated in my entire life as I contemplated the poor souls who spend each day filled with the same feelings of wretchedness and solitude as I had only just begun to experience in this icy courtyard. Almost all of them saw me, glancing out of curiosity or pity before rushing past, but only two actually greeted me. Two people out of 240 saw me as enough of a sentient being to communicate with me.

A friendly woman with a kind smile asked if I was cold sitting outside. Another, whom I assumed was a church volunteer based on her nametag, invited me inside to warm up, but I softly declined, feeling the need to remain perched until the service began. As the tide of worshippers began to slow, I contemplated the two women who had separated themselves from the wall of unwelcoming strangers to reach out to the unfamiliar, trespassing bag lady and offer a kind word. In total darkness, if even the smallest points of light shine out, they can be dazzling.

I remained in the courtyard until the last straggler had scurried into the church. Silence fell thickly, interrupted only occasionally by the muffled bellow of the organ. I knew it was time to go inside, that Gary would be starting to look around for me, but something kept me stuck to my seat on the fountain as if I were glued there. I was in a bit of shock over my less than warm welcome. I had expected this exact reaction, but I think part of me had offered the benefit of the doubt and hoped for the best, only to be gravely disappointed. At this point, asking for more repudiation just didn't seem pragmatic.

As I contemplated the disappointment I hadn't expected to feel, an older gentleman working as an usher quietly appeared as if to renew my faith in my task. With a gentle voice and soft eyes, he implored me to come in out of the cold. He silently walked beside me up the front steps and held the door for me to enter with a tender smile touching his kind eyes.

The ornate detail and expert craftsmanship of the sophisticated architecture was remarkable. Entering into such a magnificent edifice while wearing grubby rags, my hair a dirty rat's nest of frizzy curls, and mud caked on my aging face made it resonate loud and clear that I was completely out of my element.

Upon noticing my hesitation to sit among the solemn congregation that had shunned me, he respectfully motioned toward an empty seating area in the back lobby if I preferred some privacy. After I thanked him and sat down, he promptly disappeared. As we had entered the church, I'd wondered if he'd drawn the short straw and was put in charge of monitoring my every move, but that was evidently not the case. He graciously left me to my solitude. I sat alone, and although there were a few people milling about, no one seemed to take notice of my presence.

It was Epiphany Sunday. While listening to the Mass, I noticed a stack of weekly parish bulletins on a table nearby. The front page caught my attention and appropriately so. In bold letters it proclaimed: "For he rescues the poor when they cry out, the oppressed who have no one to help. He shows pity to the needy and the poor and saves the lives of the poor." As I sat in this church belonging to one of the wealthiest institutions in the world that prides itself on being "very inclusive," I was confronted by the blatant irony of it all.

I wondered if anyone in the pews would have their own personal epiphany when they hear the message of the day. Would they realize their own blindness and feel ashamed of the wide berth they gave me on their way in? Or would they listen to the sermon and walk away happily oblivious to the lesson the universe tried to teach them? I don't think it was a mere coincidence that the Mass on my first Sunday as Bag Lady had such a message. Fate works mysteriously.

I smiled to myself and rose from my seat. Gary and I had purposefully planned for a clean getaway shortly before Mass ended so as to leave the congregation members to stew over the mysterious homeless woman they'd snubbed. As I slipped out the front door, I made eye contact with Gary, who had positioned himself in the back pew of the sanctuary where he had a proper vantage point. How I managed to marry a man so willing to jump on board with my harebrained schemes I'll never know. But there he was — by my side with this as with everything else.

Taking my lead, he silently followed at a distance, strode back to his vehicle, and headed to our designated meeting place among the thick line of barren trees. Those cold, lifeless trees could no longer taunt me with their lethargic limbs — they no longer had power over me. Walking away from that church I reminisced about a much-loved hymn that was sung in every Catholic Mass I attended as a child: *Whatsoever you do to the least of my brothers, that you do unto me.* I had heard that hymn countless times, but never had it carried more weight than in that very moment. The homeless are the exact example of 'the least' described in the hymn and in the Bible, yet 237 churchgoers had all but shunned me less than an hour before. As that redolent melody reverberated in my mind, a feeling of sadness washed over me.

Again I thought about abandoning my quest. Why was I even doing this? What was I hoping to prove? The repulsive vagrant persona that I had so willingly assumed was now a cruel joke. Perhaps St. Benedict, the patron saint of the homeless, would help me out. It wasn't likely, given that I wasn't actually homeless. Clearly, I'd been living on a wing and a prayer this morning. After all the decades of my work with the homeless, I was getting schooled for the first time, and I didn't like what I was being taught.

Years of self-congratulatory community service went out the window as my intellectual eyes were reluctantly opened to the reality of rejection that is all too common among society's forgotten. Soup kitchens and blanket drives can't fix the emotional damage of being ostracized and veritably shunned. This was going to be harder than I thought.

My sadness was replaced with resolve as the realization set in: I did it! I had done what I set out to do and hadn't backed down. Satisfied with my premiere performance and confident in my ability to actually accomplish this impetuous project, I strode purposefully away from the still-quiet parish grounds. Yes, it was just a humble beginning, and yes, it was somewhat emotionally draining, but I learned more in that solitary hour than I did in 30 years of urban ministry. That morning I filled the shoes of a homeless woman and unwittingly learned valuable lessons that cannot be taught in any classroom.

As I progressed further from the Catholic church, the impact this project was to have on my simple, uncomplicated life began to dawn. I was clueless to the new challenges that awaited me at the next church and the rest that would follow. But this middle-aged housewife from the Midwest was not only fulfilling a lifelong dream but might possibly have found a way to benefit others as well. And I was on top of the world. Words declared by St. Mark pierced my naive sentiment: "Whoever does God's will is my brother and sister and mother." Farewell my Catholic family. I will not soon forget you.

Incredible relief mixed with wild adrenaline swept over me as I jumped into our car and high-fived my husband, practically glowing with excitement. One down, nine to go. We were clearly on to something here.

CHAPTER TWO

My Baptist Encounter

My philosophy is that the most important aspect of any religion should be human kindness. And to try to ease the suffering of others. To try to bring light and love into the lives of mankind.

——STEVEN SEAGAL

A man died and went to heaven. Upon entering through the Pearly Gates, he was immediately taken on the heavenly tour by St. Peter. As they floated from cloud to cloud, they came to many doors, which St. Peter would open.

The first one displayed a joyful group rolling on the floor and speaking in tongues. "These are our Pentecostals," St. Peter said.

Next, they came upon a solemn ritual of worshippers chanting a sacred text. "Our Jewish friends," he said.

Then they passed another reverent service, this bunch singing traditional hymns in perfect unison. "Our Baptists."

At the next cloud, he didn't open the door but, instead, put his forefinger to his lips as they tiptoed past. The man, somewhat perplexed, asked St. Peter what that was all about. "Those are the Catholics," he explained. "They think they're the only ones here."

Growing up as a child steeped in conventional Roman Catholicism and its presumptions, I, along with many others, believed that the Roman Catholic religion was the one true religion and that everyone else is skating on thin ice. I relished in my false sense of security while my elitist mindset pitied those outside of my doctrinal circle. Immersed in my state of nescience, it never occurred to me to question authority, so I took the strictly imposed theology I was dealt at face value and proceeded on my merry way.

For reasons that undoubtedly aligned with my juvenile logic but appear ambiguous to me now, the Baptists took a very direct hit from my perceived superiority. Perhaps it was because Baptists disregarded prayer books and icons, or because they believed in giving a sacrificial 10 percent of their income to the church, or maybe something else entirely; but whatever the rationale, my perceptions were always a bit unfair. In my delusional imagination, I envisioned the swaggering Old West, where Catholics wore heroic white hats and Baptists wore villainous black. Naturally, the Catholics always won.

As my youthful ideology gave way to adult receptive persuasion, the reality of a level playing field between the denominations became more apparent. As I developed my own relationship with God, separate from the confines of traditional religion, I came to grasp the understanding that God's ability to love the human race far surpasses all man-made dogma. In other words, there is hope for us all.

With that in mind, I greatly anticipated Bag Lady's visit to the Baptist Church. I was eager to observe the Baptists' reception of me compared to my Catholic encounter, from which I still had not fully recovered. Questions danced through my head as I set foot on the church steps on another frosty but gloriously bright Sunday morning.

How will I be received? Will I be shunned by this group as well? Will they all be wearing black 10-gallon hats?

I didn't wait around outside, because I knew from my research and reconnaissance that the Baptists attended early morning Bible study in the Sunday school room before the service. I was lost in my thoughts, heart pounding as I climbed the steps and pushed the heavy wooden doors open.

My questions were quickly answered as the church members in the lobby turned and noticed my entrance. I was immediately set upon with a warm, genuine welcome.

It was no secret that my unsuitable entrance was somewhat shocking as I stood there as the uncouth bag lady that I was, my grisly semblance with a hint of death warmed over. But this courteous Baptist family did not miss a beat. Friendly handshakes and curious smiles were plentiful. Their official church brochure said that they are "known for their love for each other, their love for neighbor, and their love for God." It went on to explain that, for that reason, they seek to care and build each other up in fellowship and compassion. Clearly this group of devoted followers was faithfully striving to fulfill this mission.

The main sanctuary was homey: not too large, not too small. The cozy, pleasant atmosphere was instantly soothing, and I could feel an undercurrent of kinship throughout the room. I sat down in a side pew off the main aisle and watched members of all ages engage in casual but affectionate conversation, lending to the familial surroundings I was happily easing into. As I observed their mutual camaraderie and responded to their cordial greetings and kind gestures, I thought to myself that I could easily get used to a place like this.

Though their demeanor was very friendly and spoke volumes, it seemed all too apparent that this dear congregation did not seem to entirely know what to do with me. I was a complete stranger in obvious and acute need. My incongruous appearance took them by surprise, and it appeared that they had no idea where to start in their aid.

What *can* one do with a homeless person that won't just be a temporary fix, a Band-Aid on a deep wound? Do you take them home? Do you invite them to go shopping for new clothes or buy them groceries? It is so obvious that the need is so great and the demand critical, but what can one do in the moment to even put a dent in such mountainous destitution?

This was a result I hadn't expected. Hostility, avoidance, neutrality, or acceptance were what I had come to gauge, but found that there were even more factors to consider in this great project. I hadn't considered observing the churches' preparation.

However, I must give credit where credit is due, as there were unsung heroes at this Baptist church who deserve empirical accolades. A group of senior ladies graciously went above and beyond to include me in conversation. Their hospitable approach was refreshing and assuaged any fears I might have had of rebuff. Doubts, caution, and uncertainty flew out the window as these lovely matriarchs helped me feel as if I belonged, even though my appearance screamed otherwise. It was clear to see that I was being loved, not judged. One sweet woman extended herself with such alacrity that she compassionately offered to sit with me during the service and drive me wherever I needed to go afterward. She treated me like a sister and a kindred spirit, displaying no shame for associating with me. Because of the forbearance of these thoughtful women I almost forgot how truly appalling I looked.

Almost.

The one and only negative response of the day came from an older woman who looked as though she had been baptized in lemon juice. With captious disdain, she frequently and blatantly glared with muted bitterness at me while seated prominently in the choir loft — a position that, in my opinion, should be reconsidered for such a person. Did I expect unmitigated tolerance and approval from *everyone* in attendance? Of course I didn't. It was wishful thinking at best, a castle in the sky. Even with the immeasurable goodwill displayed by so many who showered me with kindness, it did not surprise me to encounter at least some opposition, some dissonance permeating the goodhearted throng. There is no utopian congregation, no isolated sect of humans that has procured perfection. I felt that I could easily dismiss this trivial hindrance and still call it an overall victory for inclusion.

During the service an attractive woman stood before the obliging congregation and publicly shared a testimony about her long, grueling battle with depression. She spoke of her personal struggles with a calm, steady fluidity, and I was moved by her willingness to openly bare her soul to the entire assembly, which only affirmed their solidarity. It is often tempting for churchgoers to be so heavenly minded that they hide behind a mask of denial and erroneously portray an idyllic life, putting on airs and living quixotically, but we often forget what good can come from authenticity.

I marveled as I listened to this warrior of a woman boldly reveal such intimate, personal details about her struggle with depression. I found it greatly encouraging to witness such lucid honesty in a religious setting. It only added to my positive overall impression of this unassuming body of worshippers.

At the conclusion of the service, and in keeping with Baptist tradition, the minister extended a closing invitation for prayer, requesting those to come forward who desired to dedicate their life to God or become a member of the church. The heat was on, as if there were a big red bullseye painted on my back. I could practically feel the desperate prayers of the faithful boring into my back as concerned members were no doubt hopeful that I would eagerly jump out of my seat, rush toward the altar, kneel at the cross, and repent of the sinful decisions I'd plainly made in life.

I wanted to explain that I was just playing a role, that all was well; I wasn't really the lost sheep I spuriously portrayed. I fought the urge to reveal my true identity, my years of church leadership, to boast of my lifetime of ministry, regaling the crowd with clever anecdotes from past sermons I had preached from a pulpit much like this one. I silently longed for validation, even though in my heart I knew that pride cometh before a fall. But today was not the day for disclosure, and I was not safely shut away in a Catholic confessional where complete honesty was exempt from perusal, so I remained sitting silently in my pew.

As it turned out, though, there was no undue pressure for me to conform to their customs, and the service was dismissed punctually. The congregation members, however, lingered a while, talking amongst their neighbors jovially. They were in no hurry to leave. For them, church was not a duty but an event to which they seemed thoroughly dedicated. Sensing that I had dodged a bullet, several members bade me a genuinely fond farewell as I reluctantly headed toward the exit. In a very real sense, I hated to go. I had shared a surprising unspoken connection with this congregation, this devoted family, this loyal clan of followers, and had enjoyed the feeling of community that resided there. They were nothing like the skewed stereotype I believed as an obtuse child. These folks were the real deal.

As I stepped into the dazzling sunlight, my heart sang with thanksgiving. Favor had shined down upon me, and I was elated. It was a good day.

Basking in the glow of winter sunshine and contentment, I heard a man's voice behind me. The jovial senior pastor had apparently followed me outside and stood before me donning a cheerful smile. With straightforward sincerity he said, "Jean, the church office is right next door. If you have need of anything, please stop by and see me."

The Baptists might have been uncertain of exactly what to do with me in that precise moment, having been taken off guard, but I was keenly aware of their genuine desire to help the unconventional stranger who had barged in unbidden and disrupted their regular Sunday morning routine.

I believe that every local church should have a specific game plan in place in the event that an unforeseen need such as this arises. A destitute individual or an impoverished family could unexpectedly walk through the doors of any church on any given day seeking aid. It would be prudent to be prepared to serve the community accordingly, as providing for the physical needs of the poor is one of the most tangible demonstrations of the gospel. Churches are thought of as the harbingers of charity, so when prompted, it is important that they have alms to present. With that being said, I earnestly believe the hearts of these amicable people were in the right place.

I was in high spirits as I left that sweet fellowship of believers. Truth had overshadowed juvenile misconception as I spent the morning with a group that had treated this peculiar transient with the utmost respect. My childhood notion of religious villains wearing black hats was simply an illusion. God never intended the human race to take sides, to live life constantly choosing between "us" or "them."

The fact of the matter is this: It is of no great consequence to God to which church we belong, or if we belong to one at all for that matter. His affection for us exceeds all human entrapments and his love knows no church affiliation or religious boundary. If we will only accept his love and follow the Golden Rule — *Do unto others as you'd have them do unto you* — we are already living out God's kingdom. And then, contrary to our finite perception, the heart of God is closer than we think.

CHAPTER THREE

My Presbyterian Encounter

*Carry out a random act of kindness, with no expectation of reward,
safe in the knowledge that one day someone might do the same
for you.*

—PRINCESS DIANA

Several years ago, my husband and I celebrated Christmas on the Magnificent Mile in the beautiful city of Chicago. My nostalgic aspirations necessitated that we embrace the ambiance of a traditional holiday in a bustling downtown setting, so I insisted that we attend a midnight service in a local historic church. As chance would have it, the nearest house of worship in proximity to our hotel was an old Presbyterian church.

Upon entering the massive Gothic structure, I marveled at every elaborate component utilized to bring the holiday season to life. From the well-equipped brass section belting out beloved Christmas carols to the vibrant rows of fresh red poinsettias, I was immediately captivated. But when a large Gaelic minister bellowed out his Yuletide address high atop an opera-style balcony box, Scottish Brogue and all, I was completely enchanted. His thick accent and immense, jolly presence reminded me of the beloved cartoon character Shrek, one of my all-time favorite fairy tale characters. In all respects, my traditional holiday celebration was complete.

Consequently, the cherished memories of my Christmas Presbyterian encounter filled my thoughts as Bag Lady made her debut at the Presbyterian church from my list. In an attempt to recreate some of the comfort of my Presbyterian experience in the Windy City, for my experiment I intentionally chose one of the oldest churches in the region, dating back to pre-Revolutionary War times.

A long cobblestone wall ran the length of the property and bordered an archaic cemetery that spoke of a simpler bygone era. As I wandered past the tottery tombstones with countless names and evocative epitaphs, I imagined who these departed souls possibly were in a previous life. Perhaps they were brilliant country doctors who made house calls and were compensated with apples instead of currency or astute teachers who molded progressive minds to boldly impact future generations. But perhaps they also led tragic lives. Were they devoted mothers who died in childbirth or energetic children who succumbed to illness? I paused to consider their stories, their fates, the arcane narratives that were buried with them there — a sad requiem of all that once was. The entire campus signified the antiquity enshrined on those grounds. I breathed in the history and pressed on.

With temperatures steadily plunging below the freezing mark, and as my reminiscent ponderings yielded to the imminent assignment, I reached the front door — and that's where my peaceful reverie ended.

Whoever believes that small churches are fundamentally the friendliest churches is either misguided or naive. Less than half of the 20 adult members present welcomed me, or acknowledged me in any way at all. This was a tough crowd for sure. There seemed to be two types of church members present that somber morning: those who managed to see beyond my dreadful appearance, and those who obviously preferred not to be reminded that derelicts like me even exist.

Ironically, the church bulletin read like a laudatory textbook: "to love and serve all people, by being a welcoming, inviting, and nurturing family of faith." I guess some in attendance didn't get the memo. Sometimes, sadly, what makes it onto paper doesn't always get practiced in real life.

Years ago, when Gary and I operated a non-profit urban feeding center, we became well acquainted with a gentleman I'll refer to as Kurt. Kurt was a seasoned veteran of the street who led a bona fide vagabond lifestyle, a miserable testimony to years of destitution. What set Kurt apart from the rest of his homeless peers was the putrid odor that emanated from his haggard body. We met many impoverished individuals in need of personal hygiene, but Kurt stood out from the rest. The smell was so malodorous that my eyes literally watered every time I was in his presence.

Although his stench was not pleasant, we recognized that this poor repellant man who refused to clean up was as worthy of kindness as anyone else. So while my husband and I assumed an impervious attitude, we reminded ourselves to give Kurt the same respect, time, and attention that we gave to everyone who came to us seeking a warm meal and a cheerful smile; this was not because we are great humanitarians who perform altruistic gestures, but because we decided a long time ago that if we were going to call ourselves Christians, we'd better act like followers of Christ.

There was an elephant in the Presbyterian's sanctuary. Bag Lady did not figure into their typical Sunday morning protocol. She did not have anything worthwhile to contribute — no sparkling personality, no intelligent conversation, no fat checkbook. Why bother with someone who has absolutely nothing to offer?

I entered the unfamiliar church as a conspicuously foreign visitor and settled into a pew two rows from the back. At once I noticed something very peculiar; the first seven or eight rows from the front were completely empty. Everyone crowded into pews in the very back of the church, as if they were afraid of spiritual intimacy. I had never witnessed anything like that before.

An old-fashioned schoolhouse clock hung on the front wall of the altar. In all my years of church attendance I had never seen a clock on a church altar before. I suspected it was used in keeping with the historic theme of an old schoolhouse, as the antiquated building was probably once used by the village schoolmaster as well as the presbytery. I found the methodic tempo of the pendulum incredibly engrossing, the tick-tock cadence practically hypnotic. But from a logical standpoint it seemed counterproductive, a distraction of sorts. I suspected the regulars had grown so accustomed to its repetitive rhythm that they were no longer aware of the acutely humorous impression it conveyed to a new guest like me. I bit my lip to keep from laughing.

Surprisingly, the minister was a young, attractive woman who appeared to be fresh out of seminary. She seemed guileless and callow, impassioned with vision. Her affable demeanor was especially refreshing in a church that could only be described as mausoleum-like. As a former pastor, I knew she must have had her hands full.

During her brief sermon, the precocious minister spoke of how Jesus was publicly despised by strangers because he was from Nazareth. As the story goes, supposedly only poor, dirty things came from that distant province. How appropriate it all sounded as the poor, dirty Bag Lady sat in their midst, among their ranks, but separated still. I marveled at the notable connection and silently questioned if anyone else recognized it as well. Did they connect the dots and apply the sermon to the situation occurring at that very same moment in their sanctuary?

I wondered if anyone thought about where Bag Lady would sleep that night. Did they ask themselves when this woman might have last eaten a decent meal or enjoyed a hot shower? The simple, seemingly insignificant things in life that the average Joe citizen takes for granted are elusive luxuries for the homeless. But did they even think of it that way, or did they just not care?

All of creation tends to move in packs comprised of their own kind, continuing in the familiarity of their established habitat. Human beings are no exception. We are attracted to people of like kind, and we are naturally inclined to avoid those whom we don't understand, sometimes even fearing those who are vastly different.

One of my favorite childhood rituals was going to the neighborhood soda fountain with my grandmother after Saturday afternoon Mass. Grandma didn't own a car, so we walked up to the nearby shopping center where there was a wide array of stores from which to choose. Walking past Wrigley's supermarket, J.C. Penney department store, and S.S. Kresge five and dime, we would make our way over to Saunders Bakery. Swiveling on bar stools at the food counter, Grandma and I would happily savor every delicious spoonful of our ice cream sundaes or root beer floats. It was sheer heaven.

What was not so heavenly was the man who often sat outside of the bakery, begging for money. Terribly disfigured from a fire, he had been burnt and scarred beyond recognition; it wasn't even possible to tell if he was young or old. The fire had also claimed his vision, and his milky eyes stared blankly ahead as he muttered his pleas for aid. It was agonizing to even look at him.

I know I should have felt sorry for this poor soul, and I'm sure a part of me did. But the selfish child that ruled my conscious thought resented this man for interrupting my lovely afternoon, for the blatant reminder that inexplicable pain and suffering abides among us. Unfortunately, I was not the only one who begrudged his existence.

In the midst of this unbearable sadness, the hustle and bustle of shoppers persisted. Determined to find just the right dress for the next dinner party, decorative towels for the newly remodeled bathroom, or the latest bestseller promising to improve your golf swing in 10 easy lessons, shoppers passed by, willfully and disingenuously unaware of his plight. Tragedy had violently stolen his future and he was reduced to panhandling as a means of survival.

My grandmother, the reliable saint, never passed him by without sharing of her substance. Living on a fixed budget, she would reach into her change purse and beckon me to put an offering in his tin can, which I grudgingly did with fear. I was afraid of getting too close to this man, this victim of circumstance, even though he was undeniably harmless. I knew that helping him was the right thing to do, but fear made me hold my breath and dash away from him as quickly as possible.

Maybe the treatment I received in the church that morning was fate's way of delivering retribution. I sat alone, my own odious presence unsavory to the point of exclusion, reminded of my own past revulsion.

As the fledgling Presbyterian minister wrapped up her sermon, she implored the assembly, "Go out in the world and open your eyes to being a servant!"

I was struck again by the irony of the message of servitude while a golden opportunity sat in their immediate presence. Was this sermon merely a lesson in futility, a fruitless exercise in apathy to soothe their consciences?

I remained stoic, but on the inside, I was screaming for justice. In God's eyes, the poor and debased of this world deserve a shot at happiness too; even lowly commoners and modern-day plebeians are worthy of a fair shake.

Tick-tock went the clock. The monotonous pendulum of the schoolhouse clock grated on my nerves like a scratched old vinyl record skipping incessantly as it dared me to crack under pressure. I wishfully imagined throwing a hymnal at the ridiculous contraption and knocking it off the wall, ending its maddening, plangent echo.

The service mercifully ended. I stood, wishing to meet the young budding minister and encourage her to stay strong, keep the faith, and not lose heart. But following the benediction, she high-tailed it out of there like a bolt of lightning. Really, who could blame her? I was more than ready to disappear as well, to rush back to the comforts of home and my real identity.

But it turned out there were at least some in attendance who recognized the opportunity sitting in the congregation to apply the morning sermon. Two extraordinary ladies showed great concern by offering me a ride or money and inquiring if I had someplace warm to go. These two angelic champions of goodwill acted as rays of sunlight on an otherwise bleak day. But perhaps the most impressive display of generosity came from a young man who had been seated in the pew behind me.

As the congregation began filtering out into the frigid gale, he rose and handed me his coat with a meek smile, saying with modest sincerity, "Here ma'am, take my coat. It's heavier than yours." It was nearly 20 degrees outside, but the selfless gentleman was willing to literally give me the coat off his back. Words cannot accurately describe how profound his act of benevolence was to me. Indeed, chivalry is not dead after all. *You may go to the head of the class, sir.*

I thanked the gracious man but firmly refused his gift, feeling a sense of renewed balance and harmony working to mend my disillusionment. There really are good people everywhere; people who actually know how to love and serve; people who are willing to go the extra mile for a lost soul; people who are prepared to stretch beyond the mundane limits of rigid institutional religion and open their eyes and hearts to the needs of others.

The young man's genuine appeal stayed with me as I made my departure back through the old cemetery, pervaded with the memories of souls departed. Bag Lady's presence that morning was a test of faith demanding a response that would challenge the church body to look outside of themselves and depart from their sheltered comfort zone. *When all seems lost, hope arrives in the least expected form. What appears to look like despair in the end can very well be a new beginning. Where a dying man lies, lies hope.* Perhaps we don't need fairy tale heroes after all; perhaps we simply need each other.

CHAPTER FOUR

---·---

My Methodist Encounter

My religion is very simple. My religion is kindness.

—THE DALAI LAMA

t is common practice for actors to play characters very different from their real-life personalities. It is also relatively common for them to assume, in real life, the identity of the role they are playing. I soon suspected this was happening to me; I was becoming Jean.

Halfway into my project I noticed the line separating myself from my Bag Lady persona becoming less pronounced as I delved deeper into the character. I forewent all weekly beauty treatments, went months without coloring my hair or getting manicures, and rarely wore makeup. I no longer felt attractive and it was adversely affecting my self-esteem.

I grew obsessed, thinking of little else besides Bag Lady. I was moody and disinterested in other activities. Going out into public became an arduous chore. I developed a keen feeling of paranoia even though, in reality, I barely resembled my Sunday morning homeless character. My love of shopping came to a screeching halt. No longer did I derive pleasure from strolling through shopping malls in search of bargains and current trends. I only ventured to stores out of absolute necessity, then retreated home as quickly as possible. My husband became the designated grocery shopper in my stead. Alienated from my familiar habits, life as I knew it ceased to exist.

After walking in the shoes of Bag Lady, I began to see the world differently. Sunday morning rejection pervaded my week, leaving me suspicious of any strangers I was forced to come in contact with. Every person became the churchgoers who repudiated me, and I scrutinized each one with guarded reservation. My naturally gregarious disposition suffered as I fought to maneuver through daily activities. I was withdrawn and oddly austere, fearing that depression was taking hold.

I began to embrace the life of a recluse. The only public place in which I found enjoyment was the neighborhood movie theater a half-mile from my home, which I frequented often. The theater's darkness was my safety blanket, encapsulating me while I blissfully decompressed from my research, temporarily shelving my own project and immersing myself in someone else's story. But it was only a temporary comfort, and as the lights rose, I once again would delve into an antisocial isolation.

Putting words to the church encounters became my saving grace; it was the only lasting fix to soothe my weary nerves. As Maya Angelou once articulately declared, "There is no greater agony than bearing an untold story inside you." As I described my experiences through the written word, Bag Lady's story evolved into a quest for redemption. From a personal perspective, she became a courageous luminary, attempting to right the wrongs of a negligent society. Each weekday, I would sit down and recount her ordeal, breathing life into her adventures, chronicling her experiences and releasing them from my heart onto the page. Morning dawn was always filled with hope and promise, evenings with doubt and turmoil. By dusk I would second-guess my decision to implement this project, but nothing would stop me. My determination was relentless, my pursuit addictive. It was imperative that I see it through to its fulfillment.

Saturday nights always brought forth especially conflicting emotions. With the imminence of Sunday morning came oscillating feelings of tremendous excitement and extreme uneasiness. Gary could sense my agitation and would wisely leave me to my solitude. By now, one would presume I had naturally acclimated to my homeless role, but nothing ever made me feel thoroughly prepared for the uncertainties that awaited each Sunday. Every church and its congregation were unique and posed a different set of challenges. And each week I coached myself with a new pep talk as I suited up and went in.

My Methodist Church encounter was a symmetrical blend of positive and negative. Sitting outside near the church entrance on that cold early Sunday morning, I steeled myself for the impending predicament I had placed myself in once again. As I nonchalantly loitered alone under the dark, cloudy sky, the air was quiet, the silence deafening.

Even so early in the year, it was remarkably chilly for a Southern morning, and I could faintly smell a hint of snow. I reminisced about my childhood winters in Michigan, terribly brutal at times, yet through the eyes of a child, they were simply magical. The silence took hold and gave me a blank canvas, and I was back.

Sledding and ice-skating were customary activities for months on end. It was commonplace for every boy and girl in my neighborhood to have their own sled and ice skates. Through snowfall after snowfall, school was rarely cancelled for inclement weather; folks in Michigan were used to it. Snowmen decorated every front lawn where a youngster resided. And other than the occasional icy snowball thrown directly in my face at the hands of my merciless older brothers, I cherished this time of year.

There was something miraculous about a fresh snowfall as large snowflakes blew across the Midwestern landscape. Snow-capped pine trees and shimmering ice crystals dotted the scenery as nature decided to break out in its own winter song. In the pre-dawn hours, before morning rush hour traffic obliterated the flawless powdery fantasy and before the dirty exhaust of car fumes and pollution marred the perfection, the world was frozen in ice and time. It was like an exquisite dream, mesmerizing in all its glory.

But now it was crunch time. A horn blared in the far distance, breaking my reverie. As my unpretentious musings of youth surrendered to the tentative situation before me, I contrived an obstinate composure when the dedicated church crowd began arriving for worship. While a fair number of members acknowledged me in passing, an equal amount rejected my presence altogether. I felt as though I were in a video game where good and evil abounded, facing quandaries at every turn, the outcome unforeseeable. But this was not a game, and the Mario Brothers were not coming to the rescue. Continual rejection is an absolute reality for the homeless. Some things, like rejection, hurt more than snowballs.

The mood lightened when an affable, mature gentleman introduced himself as the senior pastor and warmly welcomed me, and some engaging women offered me steaming coffee. I could tell that their sympathetic concern was wholeheartedly genuine, and it brought equilibrium back to my irreconcilable emotions. One hospitable lady respectfully presented me with a new purse filled with useful toiletries. Obviously my disheveled appearance cried out for soap and shampoo! They were definitely prepared for an eventual visitor like me.

I once knew a homeless man to whom I'll refer to as Gregg. Although he was not a military veteran, he was known on the streets as "Army Man Gregg" because he continually wore the same green camouflage jacket, year after year. Once, while I was distributing new toothbrushes to a group of our homeless friends, Army Man Gregg refused to accept one. Even though he was clearly in need of proper dental hygiene, he obstinately informed me that the only type of toothbrush he used was Reach with firm bristles. I've had more than one laugh from that story over the years, and I assumed I looked as amusing as Army Man Gregg when I declined this kind woman's offer of evidently much-needed hygiene products.

Eventually, the parade of the brethren dwindled, and an eagerly obliging woman persuaded me to abandon my post and warm up inside. I realized how truly cold I had been as the warm air of the lobby enveloped me, a satisfying respite for my shivering bones. The kind lady escorted me into the main sanctuary, which, in the case of this church, was a spacious gymnasium complete with a colorful, aesthetically pleasing stage. Vibrant splashes of purple, green, and gold cordially inclined me to drift closer and keep an open mind. Looking around, the woman happily insisted that I take my choice of seating; she even welcomed me to sit in the front row if I desired, but I did not. The homeless are known for their idiosyncrasies and in social situations are usually introverted and distant, so naturally I sat in the back. But this darling woman was so delighted to be of service and to help me in any way she could that I was duly impressed. *A gold star for your forehead, my dear.*

Taking in my new surroundings, I assessed the deliberate cold shoulders from many. Some dared to steal a glance at my disheveled state, their reticent expressions hiding their true feelings, but I remained undaunted. I could tell they were trying their hardest to will me away.

I began to notice a recurring theme from all of my church visits thus far. The middle-aged and senior ladies were repeatedly the most accommodating towards me. But, contrastingly, women under 45 were the least friendly. The observed demographics remained quite consistent with very few exceptions. The younger women were usually polished and refined, typically accompanied by their husbands and children. Their narrowed eyes shot quick, disapproving glances in my direction only to dart away again just as quickly.

As a mother who had raised my five children to serve the homeless without partiality, I couldn't help but wonder at the example these aloof women were setting for their own children. How can a generation of compassionate adults be produced if that generation's parents failed to model that behavior? As Judge Judith Sheindlin (professionally known as Judge Judy) so adequately affirmed, "You don't teach morals and ethics and empathy and kindness in the schools. You teach them at home, and children learn by example."

Lovely contemporary music filled the gymnasium as the worship service beckoned those in attendance to join in praise. Sitting alone in a back row, I was comforted by the familiar tune of "Shout to the Lord," and fought back the urge to sing along. Forcing myself to remain in character, I recalled that most homeless people do not engage in worship but keep their guard up and their walls high. Still, the popular tune had my foot tapping.

Later on in the service, an older teenage boy stood before the assembly mid-service and bravely gave testimonial to a personal struggle. I was inspired by this young man's candor in enumerating his imperfections before the entire congregation — not an easy feat by any means! The boy spoke about how Jesus freely associated with outcasts and sinners, a practice that was, and evidently still is, looked upon with disapproval by many in the religious community. While Bag Lady's transgressions might have seemed crystal clear to the average observer, I wondered if the supercilious ones present that day considered their own artificial state of affairs while dressed in their Sunday best. After all, it's my understanding that the practice of church attendance is meant to not only challenge our faith, but to motivate us to be better people. I sat among the crowd, hoping to serve as a humble example of the more elites' hypocritical misgivings.

After the service ended, I was genially bombarded by a cluster of doting ladies who, once again, attempted to remedy my immediate needs by offering me food and money. My appreciation for them ran deep. To these generous women, Christianity was not merely a label or a deluge of lofty ideals forgotten six days out of the week. These women were living, breathing examples of Christ's teachings, and I was honored to be in their presence. I found it difficult but necessary to stand my ground and deny their lavish generosity, even though they were quite insistent.

Having newly relocated to Charlotte, I was in unfamiliar surroundings without a support network, and I wished very much to be part of their circle and call them my friends. But I knew that meeting for coffee or going out to lunch was only a pipe dream. As fond as I was of this group of older gals, it was not to be. Looking back, I'm quite certain I offended the adult Sunday School teacher who unequivocally insisted on giving me money; when I flatly refused her gift, she abruptly walked away, leaving me stinging with a great deal of remorse. But such guilty feelings were an occupational hazard of such a project.

As I turned to leave, a precious woman put forth her very best effort to assist me and humbly asked if she could at least pray for my needs. She reminded me of an off-duty nun dressed in modest street clothes with a lovely gold cross hanging from her neck. As her pleading eyes found mine, I welcomed her heartfelt prayer, a myriad of emotions flooding my soul. She looked so desperate to serve yet so resigned to my reluctance for aid. If only she knew how deeply I was touched by her kindness and profound concern. William Shakespeare said, "The eyes are the windows to the soul." Looking into that woman's eyes, I saw more intense sincerity than I believe I've ever seen. I am utterly certain that this selfless woman with such concern for a ragged bag lady continued praying long after we said our somber goodbyes.

Acts of kindness from strangers are visible confirmations that God is still alive and well on the earth. Perhaps there may be only a few people who hear his voice and obey, but those who do shine brightly. And I have no doubt that God is pleased with them.

Another Bag Lady Sunday was in the books. Unlike the true homeless, I would not be forced to scrounge around for a bit of nourishment, nor concern myself with finding refuge from the freezing weather after I passed beyond the church doors. I would retreat back to my comfortable home, take a long, hot shower, eat a delicious meal, and reflect on the events of the day and the wonderful people whom I'd met. As I returned to my sanctuary, I would shed my oppressive alter ego, hanging it up to rest until next week.

Thinking about what I'd learned from the more austere church patrons I'd met so far, I realized that maybe it wasn't such a bad thing that Jean had begun to permeate my cozy existence. Through her, I gained access into a small portal of the life of a homeless woman — a temporary pass, if you will. Most just had to rely on their own perception of homelessness to form their viewpoints, but I had something better. I had Jean. And I would be better for it.

CHAPTER FIVE

———— · ————

My Episcopal Encounter

Your beliefs don't make you a better person, your behavior does.

—SUKHRAJ S. DHILLON

'm not sure how many times I've heard the expression, "You only get one chance to make a good first impression." First impressions are crucial to guests visiting a church for the first time. It can feel somewhat daunting to show up on the doorstep of a new church as a complete stranger — an audacious gamble even. Throw a homeless bag lady into the mix and all bets are off.

One of the attributes I respect most in a church is an abundance of friendliness. Nothing will more effectively alienate a first-time visitor than an ungracious congregation with a proclivity for exclusion.

I was highly optimistic while planning my visit to the local Episcopal church. I was intrigued with their impressive website that boldly claimed they were known for their friendliness. They emphatically challenged the reader to "Put us to the test," and I intended to do just that.

The location was undeniably picturesque, like something straight out of a whimsical storybook. The historic brick chapel sat high atop a hill amidst a serene country setting. The winter snow had melted and the rising temperatures were welcome. As I trudged up the grassy slope from the neighboring commercial side property, the moist, muddy ground taxed muscles I had long since forgotten. If nothing else, Bag Lady was getting a good workout.

Foreign to a structured exercise regimen, my breathing became more labored halfway up the hill. As I continued my upward climb, I thought of an old homeless friend I will call Sam. Sam was a Vietnam veteran who lived in one of our resident shelters and was one of the sweetest guys I have ever met. Suffering from emphysema, Sam was a soft-spoken armchair philosopher who once told me "we are all just a bunch of Cheerios® in the bowl of life." As Sam's health deteriorated, he was forced to use an oxygen tank at all times. And yet, through it all, Sam never once complained. He took his last agonizing breath in our men's home, thankful for the life he was allowed to live, no matter how insignificant it seemed to the rest of society. *Sleep easy, my sweet Sam.* Remembering my dear friend, this short climb suddenly didn't seem all that difficult.

Anticipation escalated as I reached the hilltop. Parking myself on a low cobblestone wall for a brief respite, I absorbed my tranquil environment. The sun warmed my face, its vibrant rays soaking into my skin, a pleasant repose from the spell of January's winter. I considered the church's straightforward promise to reach out and welcome visitors warmly and was excited for human interaction.

My quiet preoccupation was interrupted as three smiling faces cheerfully greeted me. Choir members swathed in lovely blue and white robes stood before me. They'd spotted me as they took their Sunday morning stroll, happily sauntering about the grounds as if they had not a care in the world. Their amicable greeting and friendly manner was like a refreshing tonic. The two ladies in the ensemble spoke to me as if I were an old high school friend, and they were thrilled at our reunion. If this was any indication of how the morning would progress, I felt that I was in for a real treat.

As the old church bell rang in glorious salutation, its delightful chimes beckoning all to worship, I made my way into the charming stone church. Feeling rather sanguine, I chose a middle pew closer to the altar instead of my customary position in the back; clearly my confidence was showing.

The quaint building was small but could easily seat more than 100 worshippers comfortably. Rays of sunshine streamed through the beautiful stained-glass windows, illuminating a sublime, tranquil atmosphere. I imagined the decades of romantic weddings seen by this intimate house of

CHAPTER FIVE: My Episcopal Encounter

worship, with fanciful, dazzling brides and misty-eyed grooms declaring vows and beginning new lives. It was truly a perfect setting.

But to my chagrin, my ethereal bliss was short-lived. As the pews filled up with congregants I felt a familiar weight of foreboding settle on me. Apparently, the church's "delight to invite new people into (their) church family" was more restrictive than they'd let on, and Bag Lady decidedly did not fit into their quietly rigorous criteria. While members around me warmly greeted each other with usual cordiality, an invisible barrier had been erected around me with no welcome or greetings permeating it. It rang loud and clear that my intrusion was not appreciated. So much for a friendly welcome.

Two stylishly-dressed young women, one who sat in the row in front of me and the other in the row behind, engaged together in casual chatter while I sat between them, virtually invisible. I contemplated how rejected a real homeless person would feel in this blatantly ostracizing situation.

By now I was several weeks into my Bag Lady project, and my scruffy clothes became grimier every time I wore them. The smell of earth rose from the fibers after my earlier uphill climb, making me feel very insecure. Sitting on the plush, blue velvet pew cushion, I instantly became self-conscious of my ragged appearance. It was incredibly obvious that this religious fellowship was not as "open to change and willing to try new things" as they proclaimed on the internet.

I discreetly watched a very polished, distinguished-looking couple seated across the aisle from me. They appeared to be close to my age, and they carried a noticeable air of affluence about them. The woman was strikingly beautiful for her age and wore a subtly elegant pink outfit that painfully reminded me of something similar that was hanging somewhere in the deep dark recesses of my own closet. As I gazed down at my filthy attire I thought of my spacious walk-in closet. Shopping was my guilty pleasure, and I was the happy owner of more clothes than I knew what to do with. Perhaps my favorite Christian Dior suit would have afforded me the social status that I was denied that day.

Uneasiness prompted me to grasp for anything that would console my diminishing spirit. Surprisingly I found solace in memories of my childhood friend Jennifer. She lived down the street in our sleepy suburban neighborhood. Jennifer was raised in a devout Episcopalian household and was probably the only Episcopalian I knew on a personal level throughout my lifetime.

Unusually short for her age with an adorable pixie haircut, Jennifer was cute as a button. She had two older sisters who excelled in school and were equally brilliant. I was vastly different. I was awkwardly tall for my age, sported big, curly hair that was impossible to tame, and had two rowdy brothers who were more interested in mischief than academics.

Even though Jennifer and I were polar opposites, we made a great duo. I used to refer to her family as "the smart family." Her father was PTA president and tenaciously spearheaded efforts to increase school millage. Her mother held a master's degree, organized a school nature walk program, and was once even president of the Mother's Club at the local high school. *And* she had a heart of gold. They were all around good people and were always more than willing to lend a helping hand to those in need.

Jennifer and I enjoyed climbing the big old apple tree in her backyard, and we would talk for hours under its cool summer shade. I recall once having a tender conversation with her about our mutual belief in God among its sheltering branches. It's possible our youthful naiveté inspired us to believe that sitting high up in that tree, closer to the clouds, drew us nearer to God. What sweet innocence. Ignorant of sophisticated theology but filled with a childlike faith that could move mountains, we discussed the promise of heaven, angels, and all things celestial. Imbued with wide-eyed conviction, Jennifer and I had all the materials needed to illustrate our childish imaginings; perhaps it was simply guileless thinking. But today, in the company of these strangers in this unfamiliar church, I realized I would have given anything to be back under the protective covering of that old apple tree with my favorite tiny Episcopalian.

Thankfully mercy does have its own voice. Actor Josh Radnor once stated, "It's not our job to play judge or jury, to determine who is worthy of our kindness and who is not. We just need to be kind, unconditionally and without ulterior motive, even — or especially — when we'd prefer not to be." Therein lies my vindication.

As was standard fare, the service consisted of the usual hymns, scripture readings, and liturgical prayers. I found it ironic and darkly comical when the cantor solemnly recited a prayer "for those in homeless shelters, those who live on the streets, and those who are hungry and destitute," to which the pious assembly abstractedly replied in unison, "Lord bring peace to their souls." Was this a joke? Was I the only one in attendance who was unfamiliar with the punch line? While I regarded their impassive faces going through the procedural motions, robotically responding on cue in almost hypnotic fashion, a wave of nausea came over me. Suddenly my coveted Christian Dior suit was repulsive, and I wanted nothing to do with it or anything involving the Sunday Christian facade.

The rector of this fellowship was a robust, middle-aged woman with dramatic appeal who delivered a tour de force performance. Her speech was borderline theatrical as she carried out her sermon with enthused authority; it was unquestionably a one-woman show. Speaking to the attentive crowd that hung on her every word, she admonished them to walk in love, stressing that "the heavenly kingdom is near to those who are broken if they will turn to God, repent, and believe."

Listening intently, I evaluated why I suspect many people in this world choose *not* to turn to God. While multitudes of hurting souls steadily increase in number, churchgoers are often much too preoccupied in their own spiritual bubble to resolve someone else's need, particularly if it infringes too much on their own comfort. I was beginning to suspect that the Church at large is doing an egregiously inadequate job implementing the teachings that its members so desperately cling to.

At one point during the service, the rector instructed the congregation to cordially greet each other in Christ. I watched curiously as this highly respected church leader left her place on the altar. She strode down the center aisle, her robe and vestments flowing, and looked directly at me before passing on, quickly proceeding to the very back of the sanctuary to shake my husband's hand! Even the rector overtly rejected my presence. It became increasingly and depressingly evident how extraneous Bag Lady was to this gathering.

I have never in my adult years felt so exuberant about leaving a church. I was inundated with euphoria as I swiftly passed the sea of arrogant clergy with their plastic smiles. I was heartbroken. Not for myself — I can take it. But what about the truly broken individuals who could by chance darken this church's doors? What about the despairing ones who have nowhere else to turn? To think that they might enter this church and be greeted with hostility from the one place they might have left to turn to just filled me with sorrow. As author J.K. Rowling once perceptively wrote, "Indifference and neglect often do much more damage than outright dislike."

Halfway down the hill, a church greeter called after me, asking if I needed anything. *Sorry, too little too late*, I thought as I scurried away. This repudiated homeless woman was an after-thought, better left to her own devices, and it showed in their treatment of me. As the assemblage of the church faithfully filtered into the adjacent fellowship hall to savor their juice and cookies, I could almost see the burden of my presence lift from their shoulders. They were glad to see me go. Outwardly I was a feeble victim, but inwardly, I was a defiant crusader. I had played them at their own game. But in truth, there were no winners here.

In a dismaying but entirely unsurprising turn of events, I received an especially warm greeting from this very same minister on my subsequent visit five weeks later when I returned as a chic, middle-class visitor. Contrary to Jean's experience, my well-dressed character received smiling hopes from the now-friendly rector that I would return. Needless to say, it was a far departure from our previous parting, during which I returned her curt farewell nod with the flash of a snarky, passive-aggressive smile.

I was given a crash course on the reality of friendliness the morning Jean visited the Episcopalians. Friendliness is as friendliness does; one is only as friendly as their actions dictate. It costs absolutely nothing to be kind to someone — even to an aimless, destitute homeless woman.

Bag Lady had put this church's lauding claim of friendliness to the test, and they had failed.

First Day (Catholic Church)

At the Methodist Church

Morning before the Church of Christ

At the Lutheran Church

Before going back to the Episcopal Church

Mom and me, 2016

Pride outreach in uptown Charlotte, North Carolina

Pride outreach in downtown Detroit, Michigan

My days as a children's pastor

Biblical counseling graduation

During the Lutheran service

At the fountain at the Catholic church

CHAPTER SIX

My Church of Christ Encounter

If you cannot feed a hundred people, feed just one.

—MOTHER THERESA

L
ife experience has emphatically taught me to always have a Plan B. It was Super Bowl Sunday morning, and I was geared up once again in my homeless attire, this time planning to make my bombshell entrance at the Lutheran church. As the time approached to leave my house, I stood before the bathroom mirror and did a final inspection. As I gazed at my now-familiar disguise, I smiled and whispered, "Hello friend." Bag Lady had become as much a part of me as any other aspect of my life, her quirky characteristics and idiosyncrasies quickly embedding themselves in my very soul. As I stared at my reflection, the thought crossed my mind that this project was aging me considerably. I questioned whether or not I would fully recover. Would life return to normal after my escapade was finished? Would I even want it to return to normal? Suddenly I was yearning for more, hoping to make a difference in ways unknown to me. One thing I knew was certain: I would never be the same again.

It was the first rainy Sunday since I began my homeless mission, and it was a doozy. The downpour was steady, even torrential at times. No matter. *Into each life some rain must fall.* Deciding the stormy weather would make for an interesting twist to my story, I welcomed the rain with enthusiasm, wondering what effect the weather might have on the compassion of others.

Being a natural-born planner, I had already equipped myself with an inexpensive, clear poncho for such a time as this. The poncho proved to be a perfect accessory, both for its utilitarian purpose as well as its non-aesthetic quality, as it only added to my pitiful look. I donned my pathetic fashion statement and ventured into the deluge.

Upon arrival, however, the Lutheran church parking lot was empty. I later learned that the early service was canceled due to the weather, but at the time I figured that the congregation was comprised of die-hard football fans who declared today a national holiday and began tailgating at the crack of dawn. But whatever the case, spontaneity was the rule of the day, so I mentally arranged another visit the following Sunday. Feeling slightly miffed, I jumped back into the backseat of our car and lay down while my husband drove away.

As our Jeep stopped for a red light and I made eye contact with the passenger of a car that had pulled up beside us, laughter overtook me. What a sight I must have been! Shrouded in my poncho and lying prostrate in the backseat, they must have thought that my Sicilian husband was a Mafia hit man transporting a dead body wrapped in plastic. More than once I've heard wise guys refer to Gary as My Cousin Vinny. Well, if the shoe fits!

As the light turned green, I giggled gleefully, reveling in the release of tension. I came to treasure moments like those, as laughter helped alleviate the common stress that came from my homeless project. I developed quite a fondness for laughter and became convinced that it truly is the best medicine.

All things considered, it was turning into an interesting morning. As the laughter subsided, my attention turned to the current dilemma. I wasn't about to concede defeat and try again next week. That'd be a whole seven days wasted! I had to think of something quick. Which other church on my list was closest in proximity and time frame? As the possibilities rolled around in my head, Plan B came into focus. The Church of Christ became my saving grace.

My knowledge of the Church of Christ was limited to the understanding that they were Bible-based and their modus operandi for worship was composed of singing songs a cappella in lieu of musical instruments. Having played the accordion throughout my polka-loving Belgian childhood, even participating in state championships, my appreciation of all things musical ran deep. I was beyond curious to see how these worshippers pulled off a service without musical accompaniment.

The rainstorm ravaged the Sunday morning silence. As I exited our car a few blocks from the church parking lot, I was instantly grateful for my poncho. The rain was relentless, visibility muted. Its deliberate attack was wildly discouraging as it weakened my stamina. The ever-increasing knowledge of what the homeless endure on a continual basis again chastened me as my cloth tennis shoes squelched sadly with each footfall. With humbling comprehension, I finally understood why the homeless wear plastic bags in their shoes. After 35 years of assisting the needy from atop a privileged, comfortable perch, at long last the light went on. Reflecting on the warm, dry house awaiting me back home, my heart sank for those who have no place to call home, especially on a day like this.

Reaching shelter in front of the church doors, I paused for several minutes to regain composure and focus. I removed my soaking wet poncho and failingly attempted to drip-dry. "This never gets easier," I reminded myself, realizing that my arrival did not go entirely unnoticed. I took a deep breath and cautiously entered the building, followed by assessing eyes.

In the periphery of my consciousness I noticed that my presence was creating a stir as I sensed several church members were caught off guard by my unseemly entrance. But at the same time, I was equally taken aback. The atmosphere of this particular fellowship was very different from my previous encounters and proved to be a cognitive challenge I hadn't anticipated.

There were children everywhere — pretty little girls wearing frilly dresses, perfectly adorned with matching bows in their hair; handsome young boys resembling businessmen as they donned little suits — I soon learned that this community of believers placed a large emphasis on families, and they all sat together during the main service. The sight of children of all ages scurrying about, mercifully unaffected by the world's troubles, was both overwhelming and wonderful at the same time. I've always loved children and have worked with them extensively over the years, but I was surprisingly even more self-conscious around them than the adults. I found my insecurity peculiar because children are inclined to be less prejudiced and more open-minded than their elders, viewing life through a lens of inclusion. My only guess is that I feared my unpleasant appearance would scare them. But that was presumptuous of me, as children are unmistakably the most resilient of all of God's creation, capable of seeing the good in everyone. As innocence abounded, I gave myself permission to enjoy the sights and sounds that had rapidly become this Sunday's church encounter.

The congregation consisted of roughly a couple hundred people. As with all of my previous encounters, the members were predominately Caucasian. I was warmly greeted by around a half dozen adult members who all made great strides to welcome me. Six people out of a crowd that size may not seem like much, but I wasn't going to complain. As the weeks went on I learned to be thankful for the little gifts; every smile was a bonus. What I found interesting was that the small handful of African-Americans in attendance made up the majority of my well-wishers at this church, even though their numbers were minuscule compared to their white counterparts. Nevertheless, I felt rather welcome as the crowd filtered into the sanctuary.

I chose a pew halfway up the center aisle and sat on the end. Soon after, a young blonde woman, probably in her mid-30s, sat down next to me, along with her adorable daughter and handsome husband. She was as friendly as she was pretty, but I attributed her remarkable friendliness to the fact that her belongings were previously placed on the pew next to me and she had no other recourse but to sit there. I usually referred to women like her as Stepford wives, as their demographic were typically the least receptive to Bag Lady and typically ignored me altogether. Her outfit was simple but elegant, with not a hair out of place: the ideal woman. As tempting as it was, I resisted the urge to throw her a serious eye roll. Based on my past experience with women like this, she would, at most, courteously, if stiffly, nod at me once before fleeing my presence at the first opportunity. So her initial amiability carried very little weight with me, and I didn't hold my breath.

The congregation sang the familiar hymn, "Make Me A Servant, Make Me Like You, Lord." Perhaps my weeks as Bag Lady were making me a bit cynical, but clearly my belief that churchgoers were required to do more than just sing about serving others was justified. I was, however, impressed with their ability to carry a tune, despite the lack of support from musical instruments. As altos, sopranos, tenors, and bass leant their voices in one accord, I was enraptured by the ambience created through song. It was truly a skill they had mastered, and I marveled at their expertise.

But as the service progressed, the situation didn't seem to hold much promise for me. While the pelting rain beat against windows, the well-meaning pastor preached a sermon on parenthood with the assurance that if we raise our children 'the right way,' all will eventually be well. *What a lovely thought*, I silently chuckled to myself.

As I looked around at the young wholesome families in the congregation who listened eagerly to the promise that fruitful blessings will befall them for their obedient behavior, I grew irritable. I sat among this trusting group as a middle-aged mother of five with an empty nest who had raised my family with all the right intentions and to the best of my ability, but was met with teenage rebellion, grown children who questioned their faith, and dysfunctional relationships instead of bountiful fruitful blessings. My vast circle of church friends had all attempted their very best as well, but were often still faced with incredible heartache. The prayers of the faithful sometimes go unanswered. Broken dreams are too often a reality that even the most assiduous parent cannot prevent. And contrary to wishful thinking, sometimes life's adverse circumstances viciously burst our bubble. Life has explicitly taught me that, for the sake of self-preservation, we must cut ourselves some slack, keep breathing, and press on.

While the pastor droned on, unsettling memories from my past street ministry ruthlessly intruded on my thoughts. Memories flooded my mind of the poor children I met while assisting the disadvantaged in urban Detroit; of kids with scalp discoloration due to a lack of proper nutrition; of a small boy running to unfamiliar adults on a dangerous street corner, desperately seeking love and affection from anyone who'd give it; of a little girl who was regularly babysat by two elderly alcoholic men because her working mother couldn't afford childcare; of children who never had a chance from day one. As I sat thinking of these disturbing images, I realized how truly blessed in spades my own children were.

With a closing hymn, the service ended. As I gathered my meager belongings, the blonde Stepford wife seated to my left unexpectedly turned to me and said, "My family is going out to lunch. Would you like to join us?"

To say the least, I was absolutely stunned. Here was this sweet woman, inviting me to accompany her impeccable family to a local restaurant in an upscale neighborhood, where they would be publicly seen with a homeless person! I was acutely embarrassed at my earlier unfair assumption of her character. Week after week, I was judged unfairly by others and chastised by them, but then I turned around and did the exact same thing. While I was erroneously judging her, she was unselfishly opening her heart and making plans to include me in her busy schedule. In doing so, she was, in my opinion, a model example of Christ by denying herself and sharing the love of God with someone who could give her nothing in return. Almost speechless and with a new sense of humility, I thanked her but awkwardly headed toward the door. Lesson learned.

My path led me past the same carefree children, and as I left, I uttered a silent prayer. I prayed that life would go well for them; that tragedy would not touch their homes; that laughter would flourish; that their tears would be few. Life is a mystery that no one has mastered, and it's only by God's grace that we make it through at all.

As I stepped outside, a concerned, middle-aged woman gently volunteered to give me a ride. The brutal weather clearly worried her, as the rain showed no signs of stopping. I thanked her for her compassion as I hurriedly put on my poncho and departed on foot, undoubtedly leaving the kind woman with a multitude of unspoken and unanswered questions.

The menacing rain continued to pour down, but the harsh weather was not what was troubling me. Words from the pastor's sermon resounded in my head, as persistently biting as the rain.

I reminisced about the long years I could never reclaim, years filled with joy and sorrow spent raising my own family. I thought about how similar my youngest daughter was to the blonde woman's little girl who sat contentedly on her mother's lap throughout the service. It seems like a lifetime ago that my own little girl would ask me to play with her in the rain, to which I'd always reply with, "Not today, I'm busy making dinner," or "I just had my hair done." Too soon, her turbulent teen years came, and she shut me out entirely, no longer wanting to spend time with me at all. In an effort at reconciliation after a crushing estrangement, I once tried reasoning with her outside on a rainy day much like this one, but it had instead turned into an ugly argument that left us more distant than ever. Afterward, the wretched realization hit me: I'd finally had my moment in the rain with my daughter.

My melancholic musings revealed my own stark inadequacies. As I solemnly walked away from the church, I admitted to myself that no one is perfect. Especially me. No matter our background or station in life, we are all grappling with personal shortcomings and wrestling to overcome individual weaknesses. Each one of us is fighting a private battle, and some of us are hanging on only by our fingertips. That in itself is worthy of respect.

I don't suppose it'll take long for Jean the Bag Lady to become little more than a faded memory to the congregation at the Church of Christ, and that's okay. But if I raised even a fragment of awareness for the plight of the homeless, I successfully accomplished my goal for that church. There were some well-meaning people with good intentions in that assembly, and just like me, they deserve to be cut some slack, too.

CHAPTER SEVEN

My Lutheran Encounter

Be kind, for everyone you meet is engaged in a battle.

—ST. PHILO OF ALEXANDRIA

I t was Transfiguration Sunday, and my travels sent me to the Lutheran church on a cold, gloomy February morning. I confess that I was starting to feel a bit emotionally depleted as I, once again, sought my weekly dose of acceptance from complete strangers. I was beginning to fully appreciate the resiliency it took to survive in the extreme circumstances of homelessness, enduring inclement weather, hunger pangs, untreated illness, and incredible loneliness on a daily basis. Even their everyday tasks of seeking out food and shelter, something we take for granted, are likely more than the average person could tolerate. In the course of my brief experiment, I had begun to realize that the general public does not give the homeless nearly enough credit for the sheer strength of will they possess.

Urban folklore tells of homeless people who live underground, beneath cities in abandoned subways, flood sewage tunnels, railroad and heating shafts. Often referred to as "mole people," they are tunnel dwellers who comprise an entirely subterranean society of forgotten ones. This league of urban legend has renounced traditional culture and formed its own alliance and counterculture. Having escaped the rat race and government control, the concept of mole people has given me pause to consider the prospect that they might be smarter than we think. No deadlines to meet, no bills to pay, no hectic schedules to keep. Perhaps, in spite of their hardship, the homeless community has succeeded in escaping the restraints that traditional society only hopes to attain.

As I forged toward the Lutheran church's entrance, I reminded myself that this was not my first rodeo and that I'd done this before and would do it again. I pondered the possible good that could come out of all this — the cries of the homeless heard, the renewed understanding of Christian service for churches, and all the various lives that could be changed for the better. My hopes for an auspicious outcome gave me the courage to proceed, albeit somewhat dubiously.

There really didn't seem to be much new under the sun at this particular local fellowship, just a different label with the same song and dance. Like all the other churches, they stake their claim on "living like Jesus did, caring for each other, and serving the world." And much like the others, they provide outreach to the needy through feeding ministries that promise to be "large enough to serve, small enough to care."

Finding a seat in the main sanctuary 20 minutes early, I watched the throng of religious faithful exchange cut-and-dried pleasantries appearing almost business-like. I couldn't help but notice the cold stares from several stiff congregants, who no doubt found my attendance shocking, their immediate appraisal of my appearance turning up distasteful. Unfortunately, this reaction was becoming par for the course among many church circles. Author Annie Lobert once wrote on social media, "The difference between high school cliques and church cliques = none." But these were not immature, teasing adolescents; these were full-grown adults using their religion as an excuse to offer impenetrable stares and scornful smiles. Bag Lady had rattled some nerves.

As the crowd grew, so too did my detachment from this aloof gathering. Apart from the grand scheme of things, I detested my unkempt appearance more than they did. *Don't lose heart. This is all for a higher purpose,* I said to myself. I was reminded that I alone had volunteered for this gig with no coercion from anyone. No one forced me to shelve my organized, methodical life every Sunday to assume the identity of a hapless bag lady. So I accepted my self-appointed situation and maintained my shabby but obstinate composure.

Aside from a diminutive handful of friendly worshippers who cordially addressed me, this church seemed particularly cold. I found the exceptional aversion from this congregation to be pricelessly ironic, as I later learned their collective vision is to increase their membership by hundreds in the next five years. Considering that even my husband, who was dressed normally and was friendly to everyone around him, did not receive a warm welcome, one can fairly deduce that this group might need to modify their behavior exponentially in order to accomplish their lofty goal.

When I was a preteen in my cruelly awkward middle-school years, I foolishly arrived at the conclusion that my notably fair skin was unquestionably too pale and required immediate attention. So, in an effort to avoid further ostracism from my peers, I used my mother's foundation makeup one morning before school. This might not have been such a bad idea, but my mother's skin was a beautiful olive tone, so her cosmetics were much darker than my pale face necessitated. Only after my friend confronted me late in the afternoon did I realize that I'd spent the whole day ridiculously orange-faced. Thank God for best friends! But by then, I had made a complete fool out of myself in front of the entire student body.

Surrounded on all sides by a less than amiable church assembly, I realized that no matter our age, to some degree, we all desire to fit in. I don't consider myself an insecure person, but even I will admit that it's comforting to be liked and accepted by others. Yet in spite of this fact, I continued to set myself up, week after week, to be the constant brunt of anomalous rebuff.

Despite the truly glacial response I received that morning, one married couple did redeem my unpleasant visit. Initially, they were seated near my husband on the opposite side of the church, but when the woman spotted me, she whispered to her spouse and they promptly moved from across the aisle to sit next to me. While everyone else made a point to steer clear, these two pointedly chose to act out of love and sympathy. They introduced themselves, and I knew at once I liked them. Their actions weren't an artificial spectacle and their words held no judgment; only tender endearment came from this pair. It's remarkable how one act of kindness can make all the difference and change someone's whole perception.

The pastor's sermon piqued my interest as he mentioned bereavement and the mourning process. My emotions came to the surface as tears welled up in my eyes without warning. Perhaps it was due to the heartbreaking blow of losing my mother the previous year, or the sincere compassion from my new friends seated beside me, but whatever the reason, my guard was momentarily lowered. I thought of my dear mother, the most influential person I've ever known, and how substantially my life had changed since her recent death. In her later years, she suffered from dementia and a heart condition. Mom lived with me for the last year and a half of her life, and we were very close. She was my best friend and biggest fan. She lovingly encouraged me in all my crazy endeavors. And although she had lived a long and healthy 95 years, her death still impacted me as I remained in palpable mourning.

My thoughts shifted to the homeless and the obstacles they inevitably face when dealing with loss. Losing a loved one is difficult even under normal circumstances; I can only imagine the toll such grief and psychological trauma would have when accompanied with their existing struggles. Without the support of family, friends, and mental health care professionals, it must be an extremely arduous burden to bear. This is merely one of many battles that society casually overlooks in regards to our homeless community.

My husband and I once worked with a homeless war veteran I'll refer to as Henry. When we first met Henry, he showed little potential for independence or stability. Medically diagnosed with schizophrenia, he was practically bouncing off the walls. He lost his rights to his modest apartment and was indigent. Because of his erratic behavior, we were concerned for the other residents and hesitant about allowing him access to our residential program. But through the local VA hospital, Henry obtained critical psychiatric treatment and was able to be stabilized with proper medicine. Surprisingly, over time he became a model resident in our men's facility and was promoted to house overseer — so much for first impressions. Sometimes you have to be able to look past a person's flaws to find their hidden potential.

Due to his mental illness, it was hard for Henry to maintain personal relationships, but he was very fond of his father. He used our cell phone every Sunday evening to call his dad who lived out East. Sometimes I would overhear Henry speaking to his father, and it was as though he were an innocent boy again; the damaging effects of the war were far removed and the power of parental love and influence never ceasing.

One day, Henry received news of his father's passing, and a new sorrow was added to his already complicated life. His dad was his world, and now he was gone. Henry had lived through Vietnam, mental illness, homelessness, and God knows what else. Now grief took hold as he was forced to say goodbye to the single most important person in his life and possibly his strongest advocate. Emily Dickinson once said, "Hold dear to your parents for it is a scary and confusing world without them." I do not expect that anyone knows that more deeply than our homeless friends; while the rest of the world may turn their back, a parent rarely does.

At the conclusion of the service, the church hosted a Ministry Fair in one of the common areas in an effort to generate volunteer participation for its various outreach ministries. Interested congregants were strongly encouraged to browse along the information tables and sign the volunteer sheets. So, as the assembly was dismissed I remained behind, buying time by pretending to tie my worn-out sneakers, hoping that someone would stop and talk with me. But my brilliant delay tactic proved fruitless as the congregation silently filed past, some showing discreet agitation; their passivity declared what words would not.

The weekly church bulletin commemorated the church's quasi-friendliness by declaring that they "want everyone to know they care about them and want them to have a sense of belonging." I felt neither. I questioned how visitors are supposed to feel that compassionate promise of care and inclusion if they are scarcely even offered a simple greeting.

Of course, the sweet couple who sat with me during the service could most definitely be depended upon. With rare, genuine sincerity they made magnanimous attempts to help by asking me what I needed and offering me food. They were like streams in the desert, a welcome oasis for a weary traveler. I was curious if the pastor and church membership understood how valuable this kindly couple was to the congregation, as they effortlessly stood out from the rest. I suppose life is full of all kinds of checks and balances. This couple stood out as a diamond among stones.

My departure was uneventful. I thanked my two guardian angels for their wholehearted efforts at practicing the true meaning of Christianity as I left. On my way out, I passed the sanctimonious majority who were attending the soirée at the communal gathering, eager to decide what they could do for God. I wondered what Sabine Baring Gould had in mind when he wrote the beloved hymn "Onward Christian Soldiers." I wondered if this was his idea of mobilizing the troupes for Christian service. Stepping outside, a chilly winter blast of air confirmed my liberation. I was free at last.

Retreating quickly, wistfully sentimental memories escorted me to better days when I still had the pleasure of my mother's company, but soon turned to the unforgettable day that I lost her. I was reminded of how truly blessed I was to enjoy having Mom in my life for as long as I did. After all, some people never have the gift of knowing their parents at all, and others lose them far too soon.

Somewhere deep inside, Mom's poignant eulogy pierced my heart: *Your Mother is always with you. She's the whisper of the leaves as you walk down the street; she's the smell of bleach in your freshly laundered socks; she's the cool hand on your brow when you're not well. Your mother lives inside your laughter. And she's crystallized in every teardrop. She's the place you came from, your first home; and she's the map you follow with every step you take. She's your first love and your first heartbreak, and nothing on earth can separate you ... Not time, not space, not even death.*

Grief was replaced with solace; despair with hope; sadness with joy. It is too unpleasant for me to think of those who face the death of loved ones without the sanguine expectation of a glorious afterlife. The assurance that I will someday see my mother again, face to face, grants me the repose to firmly move forward.

I've often wondered what my mother's reaction would have been to my Bag Lady project. Suddenly I realized that I needn't wonder any longer. She was faithfully walking it out with me at every step and probably having a good chuckle along the way. Thanks, Mom ... I needed that.

CHAPTER EIGHT

My Non-Denominational Encounter

The mirror of a man's heart is his actions.

—DR. DOUGLAS WEISS

F or 12 years my husband and I were pastors of a non-denominational church in Metro Detroit. I've always found the concept of a local fellowship that is not restricted to the rules and regulations of a politically religious entity very appealing. I decided it would be careless of me not to include a non-denominational church in my research, as they make up a significant portion of the local church populace.

After extensive study, I chose one non-denominational church in particular for its evident influence in the community, as it operates several successful campuses located in various neighboring counties. Because of its familiar non-traditional style of worship, I was initially highly optimistic.

Upon entering the church property, I willed myself to assimilate to this new experience. The contemporary structure was quite massive. Numerous parking attendants directed traffic flow, and an armed security team, complete with police presence, provided surveillance. The main concourse boasted impressive floor-to-ceiling windows, an attractive bookstore, a convenient welcome center, and a trendy latte stand complete with tables and chairs arranged into a large conversation area, much like a shopping mall food court. It was official: I had set foot on the grounds of a mega church.

It had rained earlier that morning, and the sky remained cloudy and dull, despite the slowly rising temperatures. I leaned on a low brick partition 40 feet from the main entrance and waited. I was immediately spotted by two male greeters who were standing at attention outside the front doors. After appraising my arrival, they looked away and continued their conversation. This should have been the first red flag.

It was foolhardy of me to expect more from this assembly, but I am now embarrassed to admit that I did. My excitement turned to ambivalence as churchgoers began converging from every direction, many with Bibles in hand, a hum of excitement in the air. There were young couples with active children in tow; chic single women chatting; charming young men striding confidently; exuberant teenagers clustered together, giggling animatedly; there was even the occasional senior citizen, faithfully accompanied by family or friends. And everyone seemed to be in a hurry, busily racing inside the church doors as if their lives depended on it. I quickly discovered a warm reception was not on the itinerary. No one was rolling out the red carpet for this tattered vagrant. Their muted distaste was a sad dichotomy to my original expectation.

I watched a lengthy parade of worshippers rush past me as if I didn't even exist, as if I were a nameless shell of a woman with no cause for recognition, worthless beyond reason. I was Bag Lady, party of one. A few side-eyed glances were thrown toward me in thinly veiled contempt. Though the air was filled with incessant, trivial chatter, a cloud of uncomfortable tension settled over the crowd. My self-esteem was swiftly being chipped away. Everything in me craved a miracle. Was it preposterous of me to expect Christian kindness from this group of devoted churchgoers? I've been known to naively see the best in everyone I meet — at times, it's proven to be my fatal flaw. Today was no exception. The distant, abstract impression of the homeless was now a contiguous entity in their midst, and they were not pleased.

As the zealous procession continued over the course of 30 minutes, only five adults out of 447 gave me even a perfunctory, half-hearted hello — that's only 1 percent. Before I arrived, I kept thinking, "These are my people!" but clearly that was an absurd notion. Blindsided by their tepid response, I felt irrelevant and forsaken by the very ones I trusted most. I'm not sure what I expected exactly, but my fantasy was ripped to shreds. To these people, Bag Lady was nothing more than a broken-down inconvenience, a speck of mud marring an otherwise perfect day. This time my nerve took a major hit.

While the residual latecomers rushed into the building, a female greeter, eyes hopeful, cheerfully invited me inside. Although her compassion was forthright and her thoughtfulness gratifying, I had absolutely no interest in attending the service. Who would want to join a congregation of which 99 percent of the members were irritated with your very existence? This was the first time since my bag lady project had begun that I harbored such indifference toward it. With all of my high hopes deflated, all I really wanted to do was go home and lick my wounds. Someone once lamented, "I lose interest when I get ignored." And I was likely the most disinterested visitor on the church premises. But as a good sport once declared, "The show must go on."

Deflated as I was, I summoned my strength to walk into the large auditorium overflowing with nattily attired yuppies. It was time to sink or swim. I warily followed the greeter to a seat inside the sanctuary. Besides a kind lady who offered me coffee, this gracious woman was nearly the only person in the entire congregation who treated me as if I were of any value.

Although the audience was comprised of all ages, this was clearly a more modern, hipster church. The lighting was very low, and the multicolored stage lights and loud music gave the vivid impression of being at a rock concert. Over the years, I have occasionally participated in this type of religious experience, so the boisterous setting was far from unusual. But this time I was a homeless person, and I saw everything in a far different light. No amount of glitz and glamour, no amount of high-tech production, no amount of espresso and organized information booths could whitewash the true character of this impersonal gathering. They had already revealed their nature to me outside. I was not in the least bit dazzled by their performance.

When I was a child, my family lived in a sheltered upper-middle class neighborhood with an abundance of children who promised to be home before the streetlights came on. My best friend, Emily, lived down the street from me, and we played together constantly. One hot, humid summer day, Emily and I were happily amusing ourselves in the cool shade of her basement playroom when two neighbor boys joined us. As was the fad for children in the 1970s, the four of us began assembling a Hot Wheels racetrack — the orange, plastic type that snapped together. It was fun until, as kids are wont to do, the others spontaneously turned into spawns of Satan and, without warning, began hitting me with the long track pieces. I might have expected this style of roguery from malicious boys, but when Emily joined in, I was completely mortified. Being the shy, introverted girl that I was, Emily's choice to act so mean-spirited bewildered me. I attempted to defend myself but was outnumbered. As red welts formed on my bare arms, I had no other recourse but to scream bloody murder and retreat upstairs as quickly as my skinny legs would carry me.

In the company of this apathetic church crowd, I felt the same twisting blade of betrayal as I had when Emily joined in to torment me. When did the body of Christ stop looking out for one another? When did they cease to bear one another's burdens? When did they decide it was permissible to close their eyes to the needs of the poor? The heartless blows from that Hot Wheels track hurt far less than this shocking wound to my heart as I witnessed such a raw lack of sensitivity from this large gathering of Christians.

The senior pastor's appealing rhetoric certainly made it easy to apply the principles he preached in his sermon to everyday life. But what about its cosmic significance applied to the basic teachings of feeding and clothing the poor? Of lifting the fallen? Of choosing to be kind to those in need? For the churchgoer who longs to hear God say to them, "Well done, thou good and faithful servant," will their actions stand the test of true Christian service when held up to these standards? Or has religion been reduced to a rigid, decaying institution that gives no thought to a fractured humanity, instead choosing to be exclusionary and self-serving?

Gary illustrated this point perfectly when he broke the rules that day. Throughout my homeless mission, I repeatedly warned my straightforward husband not to get overly involved at church, but to keep a very low profile. I had firmly advised him to carefully avoid doing or saying anything that would blow my cover. But that morning he witnessed firsthand a wide display of stony indifference, as multitudes of worshipers blatantly disregarded me, and he could endure my rejection no longer. Prayer request cards were made available to anyone who desired prayer, and it was promised that all requests would be read and prayed for by the church prayer team. He was livid but managed to reign in his emotions and communicate them through a stern, written message:

My prayer is for you. Didn't anyone see Jesus sitting outside in rags? There was a homeless lady sitting outside while hundreds of people walked by as if she weren't there — not even a friendly "hello." The "bless me ministry" is not about Jesus Christ — it's about who I can bless. Pastor, teach your people.

My husband assumed that I would be angry with him for overstepping his boundaries, but that day I gave him a free pass. As a matter of fact, in all the years we'd been married, I had never been more in love with him than at that moment. I was flattered by how affectionately and protectively he watched over me and had sympathetically felt my pain. To him, the simple truth of the gospel lies in meeting the needs of whomever God puts in your path. For this church group it was a homeless bag lady, and they had failed to practice what they preached.

The ancient story of Jesus raising Lazarus from the dead is applicable here. As Lazarus hobbled out of the grave, he was still bound by his burial shroud. Simple reasoning would conclude that if Jesus had the power to revive a dead man, he also possessed the power to remove the graveclothes that confined him. Yet when life was restored to Lazarus, Jesus instructed the nearby onlookers to unwrap him instead. Through this incredible story, God made it clear that he expects his followers to do their part to help their fellow man. He miraculously supplies new life, and, in turn, requires them to do more than merely stand around and watch the show. They are commanded to help those who are bound with malignant weakness to walk free.

As I withdrew from the mega church, there was no need to make a mad dash for cover, as nobody seemed to notice my departure. Leaving the grounds, I simply meandered away, still bound by my graveclothes without so much as a single soul showing any concern whatsoever. While church members stood obliviously by in the parking lot, planning where they'd meet for lunch, my anger seeped in, taking root in my heart and festering. Weeks of alienation and exclusion were bearing bad fruit.

I've preached from the pulpit more than once on forgiveness and its benefits both to the giver and the receiver. But any honest preacher must acknowledge that talk is cheap. It's much more demanding to *practice* what you preach. *Physician, heal thyself.*

For 20 years I was plagued with a mysterious recurrent dream that impressed on me the importance of forgiving those who offend. Actually, if I'm being honest, it was more of a nightmare. In the dream, I owned a white bird similar to a small parrot. One day, I grew tired of him and no longer wanted to be accountable for his care. I pitilessly carried him up to my dank, creepy attic, cage and all, and left him there to die with no food or water. In the dream, several weeks passed, and I decided to retrieve the bird's body, for surely he was dead by now. But when I returned to the attic and cautiously peered inside, to my horror, my feathered friend was still very much alive. He glared at me with accusing eyes as if he could see all the way to my vile, nefarious soul. Then I'd wake up. Being a devoted animal-lover, I found the dream incredibly disturbing, as it in no way reflected my true nature.

After two decades of periodical torment, I finally had a breakthrough. One day I unexpectedly ran into someone at my local supermarket who had always been a major thorn in my side. Initially he didn't see me, so my first thought was to completely ignore him and just keep going. But instead, quite impulsively, I chose to embrace him. And as we talked, I felt those high, looming walls that had existed between us come down as forgiveness washed away resentment.

Shortly after this impromptu meeting I had my dreaded bird dream again. Only this time, when I returned to the attic, I flung the door open wide and lovingly took the bird from his attic prison and nursed him back to complete health. Then I opened his cage and released him, watching him fly into a new world of freedom.

That was the last time I ever had that dream. Author Lewis B. Smedes cleverly wrote, "To forgive is to set the prisoner free and discover that the prisoner was you."

My experience at the non-denominational church was by far the most eye-opening of all of my church encounters, and the ramifications were monumental. It shook me to my core and has caused me to reconsider many things spiritual.

It has also challenged me to be a much better version of myself every day. I decided to continuously go back to the drawing board and review how I personally help the poor from then on. I determined myself to reassess my own humanitarian efforts and reevaluate the ways I can improve my private contribution to society.

This unsuspecting congregation may have failed the litmus test for charity, but few of us do everything in our power to help our fellow brothers and sisters, and none of us ever fully do so. But we *can* choose to do the right thing. We can choose to try our best by deferring some of our own selfish pursuits and putting others above ourselves. I sincerely believe this to be the true heartbeat of Christ's gospel.

CHAPTER NINE

My Pentecostal Encounter

It's a little weird that I'm getting an award for being nice and generous and kind ... which is what we're all supposed to do for one another. That's the point of being human.

—ELLEN DEGENERES

Homelessness in the United States dates all the way back to 1640s colonial America. It was a major social stigma, widely considered by the devoutly religious as self-imposed. They subscribed to the notion that those who were not 'good Christians' brought poverty upon themselves and were reaping their just reward; the needs of the righteous were met, and if their needs were not met, they obviously deserved their ill-gotten fate. If the homeless were unable to prove their 'worthiness' to the village elders, they were callously sent away to the next town to fend for themselves and likely repeat the process again.

Unfortunately, very little has changed with the passage of time. Modern understanding frequently remains based on uninformed bias instead of actual facts. Adhering to the clichéd concept that "God helps those who help themselves," many believe that if the homeless simply make an effort to "stand on their own two feet" and stop looking for handouts, their lives will automatically improve for the better.

After decades of interacting with the homeless community, I suspect that many of its members have been given a bad rap. Contrary to popular belief, homeless people are not all drug addicts and alcoholics who are too lazy and unwilling to work. Many are college educated; many have lost lucrative jobs and have tragically fallen on hard times; many are the victims of unfair divorce settlements; many are mentally ill. But whatever their individual story, members of the homeless community are still valuable human beings who need our blessing, not our judgment.

The number of Americans living without the basic necessities of life has reached monumental proportions. Somehow in this country of unlimited abundance, a multitude lack decent shelter, sufficient nourishment, and adequate medical care. It is such a primitive life with the simplicity of no conventional responsibility, yet strangely complex in its execution. My hippie days of the 1970s, spent immersed in the drug culture and temporary vagabondage, don't hold a candle to the unsanitary conditions of the true homeless.

The Washington Post has reported that of the 1.6 million American teenagers that are homeless, 40 percent identify as LGBT. Though oftentimes many excelled in school and were hard workers, they were mercilessly forced out of their parents' homes simply because of their sexual orientation. An equally alarming number have been kicked out of churches, sometimes the very ones in which they grew up.

I have met many of these kids on the streets of Detroit, Toledo, and Charlotte. It has become an annual tradition for my husband and me, sometimes accompanied by friends, to represent Jesus at the pride parade events organized by local LGBT chapters. It is always the highlight of my summer. Our main goal is to publicly apologize for how Christianity at large has treated the LGBT community. Our only agenda is to build a bridge, to let them know that true Christians don't hate. As we pass out free candy and hugs, they often tell us stories of being driven out of church youth groups, ostracized by the very ones they thought they could trust.

We've been verbally attacked by self-proclaimed religious do-gooders who warn Pride participants to turn from their orientation or burn in hell. No wonder so many in the LGBT community embrace atheism. But from every recorded instance of social interaction in the New Testament, it is clear: if Jesus walked the Earth today, he would gladly be among Pride participants showing love too.

And while we boast of tolerance, inclusion, and heightened awareness in this age of information, society somehow still seems to be no further along in its quest to successfully remedy the plight of the homeless.

The church world has long been regarded as a supplemental vehicle in assisting the widespread needs of the poor, as many local churches have endeavored to make an integral difference in the lives of the underserved. But what happens when a homeless bag lady shows up unannounced on the front steps of a socially correct church?

It was a beautifully crisp Sunday morning as I meandered down the expansive, winding driveway of the local Pentecostal church. Tree buds announced that spring was breaking free from winter's grasp in a glorious confirmation that the warmth of nature's beauty would not be held back by the hibernal solstice. The impeccable landscape sparked my imagination as I envisioned resplendent flowerbeds in springtime with ground cover of blue and violet periwinkles or rows of red and white petunias.

As I approached the massive parking lot, I noticed an array of smiling, uniformed parking attendants ready to serve the impending stream of cars that would soon find their way onto the church premises. The building itself was very large, and there was a lovely stone patio adorned with bistro-style tables and chairs at the front entrance. It made for a very pleasant first impression.

I sat down on a low brick wall that bordered the patio and soaked in the sun. The warm rays melted away some of the Sunday morning tension that I had grown accustomed to carrying. Birds sang a chorus of gratitude for winter's pardon. It was a brand new Sunday, and I pondered what this latest encounter might bring. I hoped for the best but feared the worst.

I lost count after the first 200 churchgoers arrived. But I did not fail to notice that, once again, I was inconsequential to the vast majority who kept in step with the crowd. Aside from a few brusque hellos and assorted contemplative stares, my presence clearly held very little significance to the congregation. I was once again adrift in my own obscurity, desperately reaching for a lifeline but finding none. "Same crap, different day," I muttered to myself in weariness.

Just when I thought all was lost and there was nothing redeemable to be found among the assembly, a mature, well-dressed woman exited the building and welcomed me with a warm hug. Out of all of my visits so far, this was the first hug — an unforeseen blessing I had stopped wishing for weeks ago. Her empathetic nature spoke for itself as she cordially invited me inside and offered me refreshments. One small act of kindness and my world was set right again. I assured this dear lady that I would find my way into the church momentarily, and she walked away hopeful.

Shortly after, a young couple with two small children passed by. They clearly had their hands full, but as they prepared to enter the building, the husband whispered to his wife, and she promptly turned around and walked back to me. With a broad, genuine grin, she asked if I would like to sit with her during service. Even as I write this I am overcome with gratitude, because what many homeless people have told me that they consider their biggest struggle is not the absence of food or shelter but the loneliness. Nothing hurts the human spirit more than the feeling of being unloved and unwanted.

Sitting outside on this spectacular sunny day, the sound of the band playing songs of God's faithfulness and his unending love for mankind drifted to the courtyard patio. Although I had every intention of entering the building and observing the service, I could not seem to relinquish the appeal of my quiet solitude. With the sun shining on my back, the promise of springtime was heavy in the air, and I was hesitant to ignore it. I decided to let my feelings guide me.

While basking in the sublime moment, a gentleman I'll call Bob joined me on the patio. He pulled up a bistro chair and sat beside me. Bob had invited me inside earlier, but I suppose when he noticed my peaceful languidness, he chose to keep me company outside instead. *If the mountain will not come to Muhammad, then Muhammad must go to the mountain.* It was truly one of the kindest of gestures, because he was giving me something money could not buy — his time.

As we talked, I learned that Bob was happily married. He and his wife were raising two teenage boys, and he was a church deacon. He informed me that his deacon duties included everything from opening the church doors to plunging toilets. His candor put me at ease. He seemed equally interested in my life, asking many questions in an effort to become better acquainted with me. I sincerely attempted to answer his questions as truthfully as possible without revealing too much, but at times he could sense my deliberately evasive answers and politely backed down. A lie by omission was still a lie, and I loathed my dishonesty, especially with someone as kind as Deacon Bob. But I held out hope that the end would justify the means.

Bob and I spent a wonderful hour talking about many things, from religion to sports to travel. His enthusiasm for life and his concern for others was inspiring. Instead of taking a clinical approach toward me, he was moved by the heart. He displayed what I refer to as perfect goodness — the kind of goodness that one with an acute need would understand.

Throughout our genial conversation my emotions fluctuated from sadness to happiness, stopping everywhere along the way — every capricious response was open to me. The fact that this kind man viewed a penniless bag lady as worthy of his valuable time was humbling. I'm sure there was a whole list of responsibilities demanding his attention, but he chose me instead. As church members walked past us I no longer felt subconscious — I was with Bob. Author and motivational speaker Jim Rohn once said, "One of the greatest gifts you can give to anyone is the gift of attention." Deacon Bob accomplished that and so much more.

As the church service ended and congregants slowly began exiting the building, I regretfully walked away from Deacon Bob as if I were bidding a final farewell to an old friend. I longed to apologize for my deceit, to explain my true intent. I hoped he would someday realize the magnitude of his actions and the impact they made on this lonely homeless woman.

I eluded the vigilant parking attendants by dodging in between the sea of parked cars until I found my husband. On the drive home, Gary and I had our usual exchange of stories. He couldn't say enough nice things about the church or the friendly people who worshipped there, as he had attended the entire service and had met many neighborly people. I was confused to say the least, as my experience with the general crowd outside was much different. *Sorry, dear, the jury is still out on that one.*

I was tempted to launch into a diatribe of rebuttal, adding closing arguments to my case. But in an attempt to appear impartial, I considered his sagacious viewpoint. I truly wanted to believe the best in this congregation, as my husband was obviously convinced of their virtue.

In good conscience, I conceded that there was something that caused this particular encounter to stand out from the rest. Maybe the average churchgoer feels a sense of helplessness when confronted by a homeless person's unexpected presence. Perhaps the means to help are present, but the wherewithal to spontaneously implement those means is lacking. In fact, Deacon Bob had informed me that a team of church members house the homeless on site every Thursday night in a grassroots effort to serve. So why do so many church people still cringe at the sight of a defenseless bag lady?

Throughout my years of ministerial leadership, I have noticed a recurrent theme. No matter its size, there is usually only a small percentage of members in every fellowship who perform all the necessary duties required to sustain the church's operations. I think it's reasonable to assume that those faithful few are often overshadowed by the masses who show up on Sunday morning. The forest can be lost through the trees in these cases. But to effectively represent Christ on a mass scale, it will require more obliging members to stretch outside of their comfortable boundaries and take care of God's business.

Regardless of personality type, anybody can extend themselves to be kind at the very least. This should especially be true of avid church attendees. And even though everyone is not wired to be as outgoing and extroverted as Deacon Bob, even just a friendly hello can make a difference.

As English cleric and poet John Donne so aptly penned, "No man is an island, entire of itself." Despite sexual orientation, social, ethnic, racial, or religious affiliation, we are all connected to each other.

Although I neglected to darken the doors of the Pentecostal church that Sunday, I *found* the church on the patio that morning. I did not sing a single hymn or pray one prayer; I failed to hear a formal sermon or a Bible verse recited. But God was on that patio because someone who saw a need cared enough to bring church to me — someone who valued the poor more than their own agenda; someone who put a stray homeless person before all else. And that is, unequivocally, what church is really all about.

CHAPTER TEN

My Church of God in Christ Encounter

*Nothing is black or white, nothing's 'us or them.' But then there
are magical, beautiful things in the world. There's incredible
acts of kindness and bravery, and in the most unlikely places,
and it gives you hope.*

—DAVE MATTHEWS

t behooves me to say that in spite of my diverse experiences as Bag Lady, one church ultimately shined above the rest. Therefore, I have chosen to save the best for last.

My spiritual involvement with the African-American community has been consistently positive. In fact, my husband and I were pastors of a bi-racial church in Detroit for years and have made many friends of color. I've always been a firm believer in the power that racial unity has to evoke social change. So when a black church emerged on my radar of potential choices, I jumped at the opportunity to include them in my research.

To lend credence to my convictions, I am of the persuasion that African-Americans are some of the friendliest, most actively caring people God graced on this Earth. Their uninhibited personalities and zest for life never cease to amaze me. Their very presence is capable of lighting up a dull room. With that being said, I was still completely unprepared for the extraordinary response that Bag Lady was about to receive.

To all outward appearances, the Church of God in Christ was somewhat intimidating. The towering palatial structure made me feel like it was scrutinizing my every step as I drew closer to its grand entrance. Suddenly I knew what Dorothy felt like in the Emerald City as she fearfully approached the Great Oz. My base instincts kicked in, and for an instant, I contemplated a hasty retreat, but it was too late to be overtaken by cowardice. I reached for the big, heavy door and crossed the threshold.

Upon walking through the doors of this elegant building, I was welcomed by a greeter, a vivacious woman dressed in white from head to toe, beaming from ear to ear. What surprised me most was her immediate response. There wasn't a trace of hesitation in her welcome. She didn't flinch, frown, or look confused even for a second. It was as though she had been expecting me, and my entrance thrilled her beyond measure. The tense, unsure knot in my stomach immediately unwound with her exuberant greeting. She opened her arms wide, embraced me, and planted a big kiss on my cheek! For me this was the pièce de résistance. Here was this gorgeously attired black churchwoman hugging this disgusting, grimy white bag lady, without the least bit of reticence.

I nearly broke down in tears right there on the spot and confessed to everything! It is customary for church people to speak of loving the unlovable, but it's quite another thing entirely to actually do it. In that moment, this lovely woman was living out the gospel of Jesus Christ that so many churchgoers claim in word only. *Toto, I have a feeling that we're not in Kansas anymore.*

Eventually I pulled away from this precious woman and apologized for getting her beautiful outfit dirty, to which she dismissed my remorse with a wave of the hand that impressed I was the only important part of the equation. I was awestruck at the level of respect that she bestowed upon me and was blown away by her buoyant welcome. I longed to warm up to her friendship and share a conversation, but the typical homeless person is far from social, their lives scarred from years of abuse and neglect. They trust no one. So while my visceral feelings were flying high, my incognito charade continued.

My encounter that day was unparalleled to any other. Words cannot begin to describe the overwhelming reception I received and absolutely reveled in. Hugs, handshakes, heartfelt greetings — these church members held nothing back as they treated me more like a noble dignitary than a homeless vagrant. One sweet lady invited me to sit with her, to which I contritely declined. Another well-meaning woman inquired about any needs I might have that she could pray for. My amicable morning continued in this manner.

Throughout the worship service, I was repeatedly brought to the brink of tears. I was elated at the warmth and affection I received in spite of my frightful appearance. It's no secret that African-American women have cornered the market on hair care. Their style expertise can tame the coarsest hair into a meticulous work of art. I can only guess what they thought of my matted mop that must have made them think I'd had several rounds of electric shock therapy before the service.

My parents were married for 20 years before they began adopting children. Why they didn't decide to forego raising a family and spend their money gleefully sailing around the world, I'll never know. But out of the goodness of their hearts they became first-time parents in their 40s.

Mom and Dad transformed into the most devoted parents on the planet. They decided that one of them should be home when my brothers and I returned from school each afternoon. So while I was still an elementary student, my dad took advantage of early retirement after 30 years at Chrysler. He became our primary caregiver while my mother continued working at the local hospital. Dad could cook meals and clean house better than any traditional homemaker on the block. He was also an artist and a licensed upholsterer, and enjoyed various domestic hobbies. My curly hair became one of his favorite hobbies.

My paternal birth family had strong African-American roots, so naturally, I was endowed with some of their African-American attributes. As luck would have it, all of those attributes ended up on the top of my head.

Every morning before school my dad, armed with a spray bottle, would sit me down in the bathroom for nearly an hour and fix my hair. Instead of flattening down my frizz, he accentuated it, spit curls and all. I hated it with a vengeance, but hey, the old ladies in the family loved it. I should have been grateful to have a dad who cared this much, who took an incredible amount of time out of his demanding responsibilities to give me his undivided attention, but I was mortified at the masterpiece he unveiled in the bathroom mirror every single morning. I was a nappy-headed geek living in a Marcia Brady world. I have no idea how I survived childhood.

Humiliated beyond measure, I was the frustrated Sarah Jane from the movie "Imitation of Life", the light-complexioned girl who passed as 100 percent white, living in a segregated, prosperous, all-Caucasian world while silently screaming, "I'm white, dammit!"

But as I sat in the Church of God in Christ congregation that morning and looked around appreciatively, scanning the faces of these compassionate black brothers and sisters, I was deeply humbled. The impulse to move in and adopt every one of them was compelling, for they genuinely treated me like family. Was this all a mirage or was it actually happening? The aura throughout the congregation was so unified, the rhapsodic cohesion remarkable. I never wanted to leave.

Relishing the warmth of unbiased acceptance, I recalled a little boy from grade school named Dante. Dante lived in the children's foster care group home, a facility located near my school in the upscale neighborhood of Grosse Pointe, a veritable land flowing with milk and honey. The group home stood out like a sore thumb among rows of "Leave It To Beaver" homes and manicured lawns. The kids from that home were wards of the state and wore shabby clothes — pants that were too short and mismatched outfits — that I now find absurd given the extreme wealth in the community. It seemed cruel to throw these children into the social mix where polo shirts and cardigan sweaters were the norm.

What made life harder for Dante was the fact that he was possibly the only black kid in an affluent, all-white neighborhood during the still highly segregated 1970s. Some of the white boys in our classroom would frequently crack insensitive racial jokes, but Dante would just smile and shrug it off. If it bothered him, he never showed it. As an inconspicuous mostly white kid with no readily apparent social challenges, I was spared from and oblivious to Dante's daily struggles.

Seated in church alongside this amazingly impartial crowd of African-Americans, I was bitterly embarrassed by the injustice of it all.

In his sermon, the minister spoke about choosing to be great and practice living in love and peace — their main goal was to be a church that reaches out in love to the world. What I found to be empty words in some churches was put into immediate and unapologetic practice in this place.

As morning turned into afternoon, I sadly realized that my time among God's faithful at the Church of God in Christ was drawing to a close. My disappointment was soon replaced with the concern that I wouldn't be able to execute my standard smooth getaway due to the churchgoers' sincere interest and kindness towards me. But as providence would have it, I happened to be visiting on Communion Sunday, a sacrament this congregation observed only once each month. So while the members eagerly headed toward the front of the church to receive communion, I discreetly headed toward the back. I made a beeline out the front door and began my departure down the long driveway at an unusually fast clip, triumphant in my swift footwork.

But my great escape was short-lived. I was hardly 100 feet down the drive when I heard a woman's voice call, "Ma'am, would you please come here?"

I froze and grudgingly looked behind me. One of the female ushers was standing at the door, beckoning me to come back. "Shit!" I whispered to myself as I backtracked, my self-confidence draining. I felt as though I were a timid schoolgirl who had been caught sneaking out of school.

My apprehension only intensified as she gestured for me to follow her back inside the front lobby where a solemn-looking security guard was standing watch nearby. He reminded me of Byrd, the stoic, rigid bailiff from "Judge Judy." Was I under arrest for vagrancy? If there were laws against that, I was unaware of them.

Before I could speak, the usher said, "Ma'am, do you have any place to stay? Perhaps you need a ride somewhere — it's cold out there!" Relief flooded through me. I tried to assure her that I was perfectly fine and that walking was an enjoyment. She proceeded to tell me that the church people had raised a special offering and they wanted me to have it!

Now I found myself in quite the predicament. Pangs of guilt permeated my thoughts as I realized the compassion of the souls who were willing to go to such great lengths for a stranger in need. I momentarily lost all focus. In my shame I was thinking, "I'm going straight to hell for this!" But I reined in my emotions and reminded myself that my role as Bag Lady was for the greater good, and I needed to finish the work I had started.

Suffice to say I longed to hug that usher profusely for her generosity, but I repressed the impulse and merely thanked her, refusing any help.

Despite my best efforts, this determined woman was not about to give up that easily. She studied me with concern and asked, "Do you have somewhere to sleep?" Finally, an uncomplicated question! But even when I answered with an emphatic "Yes!" she did not appear even remotely convinced.

"You don't have a hat or gloves!" She inspected my pitiful clothing with a look of intense dismay. I showed her that my flannel jacket included a hood, and I covered my head with it as I slowly inched back toward the exit. I made one final attempt to put her mind at rest by explaining that I'm from the North and can handle the cold. The sweet, caring usher looked woefully resigned as I made my way outside once again, thanking her as I departed.

The Church of God in Christ family exceeded all my hopes and dreams for a favorable outcome. They were the summation of all that was good at my previous encounters, and then some: the Catholic usher who mercifully gave me shelter, the Baptist ladies who treated me with the kindness of a sister, the young Presbyterian man who generously offered me his coat, the Methodist friend who prayed for me, the young blonde woman at the Church of Christ who invited me to dine with her, the Lutheran couple who faithfully stood by me in friendship, and Deacon Bob's benevolent companionship at the Pentecostal church.

Throughout America's relatively short history, racial prejudice has left an ugly stain on humanity. From the horrors of the African slave trade, to the violence of the Civil Rights Movement, to the tensions surrounding Black Lives Matter, hatred and division have separated the people of our country. But I found no separation or discrimination that day as I delighted in the presence of my black brothers and sisters. They did not recount the atrocities thrust on their ancestors, nor the injustices they currently face. I was the minority, yet they refused to remind me. I was in their space, yet they looked deeper than the color of my skin and chose love instead. The seemingly idealistic solutions that are often discussed in political platforms, civic conferences, and public symposiums were effortlessly demonstrated by this impartial congregation. I was the vulnerable beneficiary of unbiased acts of compassion, and God was smiling.

My heart was full as I joyfully strolled away from the wonderfully rare fellowship of people who worshipped within the no-longer-intimidating church. Faith in humanity and racial unity are alive and well if we are simply open to the possibilities. My brain was playing an endless guilt trip like a broken record, but my heart thundered its message loud and clear: I had just witnessed a little piece of heaven.

EPILOGUE

In an effort to enjoy a happy, contented life, I have a propensity to believe that most people are relatively good. Walking in the shoes of a homeless person has certainly challenged that theory.

During my role as Jean the Undercover Bag Lady, I met some wonderful church members who passionately resembled the epitome of empathy and mercy, exemplifying sincere generosity in word and deed. They were the embodiment of everything that is right in this world. Their sacrificial love and support made all the difference as I carried out my project. Unfortunately, based on Jean's experience, these kind souls appear to personify only a small minority of the masses who attend church on Sunday morning.

My research suggests that many in the church world might be more entrenched in the traditional rigidity and dogma of religion to allow their natural moral compasses to point north. Firmly established religious practices and patterns seem to have taken precedence over Christ's command to love our neighbor as ourselves. However, true Christian character does not lie in abiding strictly by a puritanical set of rules but by literal, pragmatic application of its basic tenants.

As Gandhi so eloquently said, "I like your Christ, I do not like your Christians. Your Christians are so unlike your Christ." After examining the conclusions from my Bag Lady experiment, I tend to concur with his perspective.

Christ ordained the Church to be his representatives on Earth. If its response to Bag Lady is any indication of its overall performance, his church is failing miserably. During my undercover work, I was confronted repeatedly with a phenomenon that I have coined "Ferris Wheel Religion" —

performing the same circle of religious duties over and over but never really getting anywhere. Sitting among the religious faithful, partaking in the ennui that constitutes a great deal of their Sunday morning, I gazed around the room at all the lovely worshippers, their blank, staring faces praying to a God they have never met.

As my project evolved, I found myself changing my personal label from Christian to believer; suddenly I no longer felt very Christ-like. My own shallow competence of the homeless became flippantly manifest. Yet I have never felt so honored to represent a group of people or to be involved in such a worthwhile project.

Many churchgoers will gladly travel on an overseas mission trip or financially donate to an inner-city fundraiser, but few will take the small step to welcome the poor and destitute into their own churches. Preferring that these offensive outcasts remain at a comfortable distance, far from their pristine, impeccable neighborhoods, they would rather choose to have the homeless sequestered in their own filthy world, hidden away from the day-to-day rituals of mainstream society. From a safe distance, they can imagine themselves sympathetic without having to experience any of the potential discomfort of an authentic interaction. But where prejudice is allowed to incubate, true Christianity cannot thrive.

As they say, you only have one chance to make a good first impression. As evidenced by the Bag Lady experiment, a local fellowship typically only has one opportunity to welcome and help a homeless person who walks through their doors. It is likely that the homeless person will never return again, which might be further determined by the reception that person received on their arrival. Although this prospect may delight a number of congregants that is *not* how Christ intended his followers to react.

Jesus spoke about this in Matthew 25:40: "Whatever you did for one of the least of these my brothers and sisters of mine, you did for me." When you reject the poor and thrill in their departure, you reject Jesus.

Churches are sanctuaries in the most literal sense; they are places of refuge and safety. They are meant to be a safe haven, a place for the weary to find rest. But I found it impossible to find refuge in most of the churches I visited as a homeless woman.

With that said, my objective with this experiment is not to instigate a tirade against the world of Christian churches, but rather to shed light on some possible solutions. I believe religious circles can rise above their inadequacies and be an accurate representation of Christ. And I am convinced that change begins with church leadership, as it is the most influential component in the spiritual community.

On a larger scale, a cohesive ecumenical movement is necessary, where churches of all denominations lay aside their theological differences and join together for a greater purpose. Sectarian factions have divided the Christian world for ages and have hindered humanitarian efforts. While religious sects have debated doctrine and liturgy, humanity continues to suffer. Someone once said, "Let us feed the hungry, house the homeless, stop the killing, and provide medicine for the sick. When we have accomplished that, we can sit around and argue about religion." Until religious diversity coexists with constructive unity, charitable productivity will remain below par.

On a local level, it's my experience that far too many church leaders have remained removed and detached from the practical needs of others. I don't mean to promote anti-clericalism by any means, but I feel that many leaders have permitted their rank in the upper echelon of church hierarchy to isolate themselves from the common people. But in my opinion, if ministers do not possess the capacity to be accessible to the masses, even to impecunious strangers, they have no business overseeing a church.

Out of the 10 churches I visited as Bag Lady, only three pastors approached me and introduced themselves. As a former pastor, I am aware of the responsibilities of managing a ministry. I also understand the enormity of the financial pressures they face. But instead of concerning themselves with how much money is in the offering plate, it would be prudent for leaders to teach their flock how to mirror Christ *through their example,* perhaps by implementing hands-on programs to assist the needy in their surrounding communities, by welcoming the poor with open arms into their own congregations, by being the first to jump in and help the less fortunate physically, emotionally, and spiritually — not for the praises of men, but for the glory of God.

I learned the value of clerical transparency firsthand in my early years of church leadership. Prior to our Sunday evening service, a very sullen, destitute young woman walked into the non-denominational church at which my husband and I pastored. I sat down beside her and instantly sensed her walls go up, the protective invisible barrier that many home-less people erect in the presence of clergy. Like so many others who have been disappointed with the Church, this woman assumed that my life was made up of nothing more than a sequence of blissful events. Who was I to understand her situation without judgment? I must have obviously been there only to tell her to repent of the wicked ways that brought her to destitution.

In an effort to convince her that I was not born with a silver spoon in my mouth and was there to connect with her and help, I felt compelled to share with her a sad and private story from my own past. Immediately her countenance changed. Because I was genuine and obviously authentic with her, her defensive walls came tumbling down, and she openly discussed her dismal situation with me. She knew that I was willing to reach past her boundaries to embrace her, and it made all the difference. If such a simple moment of sincere effort could serve someone so effectively, imagine what we could do with prolonged, thoughtful service as an entire church body.

In keeping with the teachings of Christ, when leaders dismiss the peck-ing order and actively embrace the actions of a humble servant, the congre-gation will naturally follow suit.

Furthermore, I believe it's imperative that the vast majority of church members stop just playing church as if they are performing a role, but start actually *being* the Church. Christianity was not established to be a self-in-dulgent social club where exclusive cliques come to be seen going to chapel. If church members refuse to elevate their hearts to *everyone* who walks through their church doors and offer no intent to reach people outside those doors, they have grossly neglected the true purpose of being a Chris-tian. Aside from bake sales, chili cook-offs, prayer breakfasts, and knitting clubs, self-professing believers have a definitive job to perform. And if they refuse to do it, God will find someone else who will.

Population records confirm that nearly 2.2 billion people globally identify as Christian. Despite this fact, it remains obvious that not every-one who calls themselves a Christian is the genuine article. Christianity should not merely be used as a convenient label, but as an expression of faith *and* works. As stated in the book of James, "Faith without works is dead." If one cannot prove their faith through their attitude and deeds, their religion is useless.

By its very nature, one cannot persuasively refer to themself as Christian without actual evidence. John 13:35 says, "By this everyone will know that you are my disciples, if you love one another." Yet a substantial portion of society from all walks of life continues to avoid church attendance in record numbers. Why is that? English novelist Graham Greene perceptively wrote, "They are always saying God loves us. If that's love I'd rather have a bit of kindness." In all likelihood, it appears expedient for the Church to begin examining themselves on a deeper level, for they are clearly missing something of considerable importance.

Just like in the theory of six degrees of separation, the whole of mankind is only a few steps apart from each other. Like it or not, we are all connected on a deeper level. And when the Church removes itself from the plight of the poor and homeless, when they cease to welcome them into their fold, they remove themselves from the call of God.

Simply speaking, the human race is looking for authenticity in religion; they are seeking a place to belong. From country clubs to biker gangs, people strive to be part of something bigger than themselves; they desire a sense of family. It's not too late in the game for Christian churches to assume their responsibility and love *all* of humanity without stipulations or hidden agendas. And because the homeless community ranks lowest on our culture's priority spectrum, it is crucial that there be an organized, collaborative effort to ensure their well-being — why not spearhead that effort as the Church? Father Gustavo Gutierrez said it best: "So you say you love the poor? Name them."

The bottom line is this: the world is not impressed with the number of Bible studies one frequently attends, nor one's efficiency at quoting scripture. If a devout churchgoer puts only minimal effort into helping their fellow man, their faith is worthless.

No matter your religion, or lack thereof, we are our brother's keeper.

And the behavior of the self-proclaimed Christian world is being watched and judged scrupulously by the rest of humanity. Perhaps that is of little significance to the stereotypical church member whose only goal is to punch the clock and be seen in church on Sunday morning. But for those who desire to "be the change you wish to see in the world," I hope you will begin today and try to make the world a little brighter for someone — perhaps even a homeless bag lady.

ACKNOWLEDGMENTS

———— • ————

To my Heavenly Father, who always sees the best in me, even when I don't.

To my hunky husband, Gary, who has been my devoted partner in crime for the past 40 years. I could not have done life without you.

To my brilliant children, Madonna, Sheila, David, Michael, and Chelsea, who constantly keep me on my toes. I'm proud of every one of you!

To Ronnie, my beloved sister from another mister, and Beth, my hilarious BFF, who have graciously supported me throughout this endeavor. Your encouragement has made the difference.

To my beautiful niece, Heidi, for reading my very first manuscript and giving me the courage to go for it.

To my editor, Katie Cline, and the entire team at Atlantic Publishing who patiently guided this technophobe newbie through the publishing process.

To my multi-talented daughter-in-love Amanda, for standing out in the rain to shoot my cover photos.

To all the many friends and prayer warriors who prayed this project through to fruition. You know who you are, and you're appreciated.

And to the millions of homeless brothers and sisters worldwide. You are not forgotten.

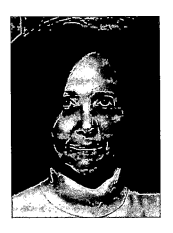

ABOUT THE AUTHOR

Kimberly Bowman has worked in various capacities with homeless ministry and church leadership over the past thirty years, including founding a nonprofit that has served the homeless community since 1996. She relishes in new adventures and takes immense pleasure in sky diving and zip lining. She lives near Charlotte, North Carolina with her incredibly tolerant husband, Gary, and her spoiled-rotten schnauzer, Bruce.

Kimberly Bowman is a motivational speaker who enjoys inspiring others to jump-start programs that help the homeless and disadvantaged in their communities. If your church or civic group is interested in booking her for an event, you can contact her through her Facebook page at Undercover Bag Lady.